*The Administration of
Public School Personnel*

THE LIBRARY OF EDUCATION

A Project of The Center for Applied Research in Education, Inc.

G. R. Gottschalk, Director

Categories of Coverage

I	II	III
Curriculum and Teaching	Administration, Organization, and Finance	Psychology for Educators

IV	V	VI
History, Philosophy, and Social Foundations	Professional Skills	Educational Institutions

The Administration of
Public School Personnel

HAROLD E. MOORE

Lecturer in Education
Arizona State University

The Center for Applied Research in Education, Inc.
NEW YORK

Foreword

Recruitment, selection, orientation, assignment, transfer, promotion, and separation of staff—these are traditional and proper concerns of the staff personnel administrator in schools as well as in other complex, formal organizations. They represent the normal flow of the staffing function. Since school personnel are public employees, the personnel administrator must have a special knowledge of the law as it pertains to these employees. In addition, he must have an awareness of the ethical and economic relationships involving the school staff.

But if these activities and areas of knowledge are his traditional concerns, they are not the most urgent ones in these times. Rather, it is the pressures and tensions contingent upon maintaining good morale among the personnel; appraising personnel job performance; allowing for collective bargaining and other professional negotiations; coping with strikes and government sanctions that beset and upset the personnel administrator. His very role in the power structure of the school system with the accompanying pressures and tensions constitute his challenges and bring on his headaches. If they are to become challenges rather than continuing headaches, it is because he has developed a philosophy of administration and has a conceptual view of the organization and functions of the staff personnel segment of the *total* school organization, thus giving him a more perceptive appreciation of the inter-relationship of individuals and the total organization.

For both the general school administrator and the personnel specialist, for both the neophyte administrator and the veteran, this book written by a nationally recognized authority in the field provides added knowledge and a comprehensive overview of both traditional and current topics in the field of school personnel administration.

Since no one book could encompass the whole scope of staff

personnel administration in schools, readers are referred to two other volumes in the Library of Education Series which treat other aspects of the field: *In-Service Education for Teachers* by John C. Moffitt and *Staff Welfare Practices in the Public Schools* by Leslie W. Kindred and Prince B. Woodard.

RICHARD C. LONSDALE
Head, Division of Administration and Supervision
School of Education
New York University

The Administration of
Public School Personnel
Harold E. Moore

Professor Moore has written a comprehensive yet succinct text on the range of problems encountered in administering personnel in the public schools of America. As in all organizations, recruitment, selection, placement, promotion, remuneration, and motivation of staff members are extremely important and often involve many difficulties and challenges. This volume offers the practicing administrator help in solving his personnel problems. To help the student of administration it defines clearly the personnel problems of public schools.

The author sets forth the basic characteristics of school personnel administration by discussing its philosophy, then gives a presentation of its historical development as well as its function. His presentation of the principles of personnel administration is followed by an annotation of appropriate procedures to follow. Chapter III is a comprehensive statement of the organization and function of the many roles that exist in the school system. Dr. Moore considers the morale problem, the difficulties of appropriately recognizing the efforts of staff members, and the need for coordination of school personnel. The extremely important functions of the recruitment, selection, and orientation of staff members are handled in a highly competent manner.

Many aspects of changes in employment status are discussed briefly but comprehensively. The final two chapters deal with ethical, economic, contractual, and staff relations.

This book should be read as one of a "cluster" of Library of Education books dealing with personnel. *School Law* by Warren E. Gauerke, *Staff Welfare Practices in the Public Schools* by Leslie W. Kindred and Prince B. Woodard, *Organization of Public*

Schools by D. Richard Wynn, *In-Service Education for Teachers* by John Clifton Moffitt, taken together with Moore's book, give the reader an excellent presentation of the many facets of school personnel administration. *Personnel Administration*, written last, was planned in such a way as to make the "cluster" a comprehensive treatment of the diverse problems within personnel administration.

DANIEL E. GRIFFITHS
Content Editor

Contents

The Administration of
Public School Personnel

CHAPTER I

Introduction to School Personnel Administration

The strength and effectiveness of a school system is largely determined by the adequacy and quality of its staff. Recognizing this fact has led the total administrative process to be greatly concerned with personnel policies and practices. School systems, writers and researchers in education, business and public administration have all contributed to the rapid development of the body of knowledge behind what is known as school personnel administration. Summarizing the progress, status, and trends in this area has become the undertaking of this publication.

An Administrative Function in Transition

Changing concepts of personnel administration. The numerous activities associated with school personnel administration have as their basic purpose facilitating the educational objectives of the school system. Especially since World War II the changes in the nation, and, for that matter, in the world, have been so rapid and drastic that all institutions have been hard put to adequately perform their functions in society. The schools have been taxed to the utmost with a burgeoning population and by new social and educational roles, and by all kinds of pressure groups desiring them to serve special and often biased purposes.

Since the schools function through their staffs, school personnel administration is naturally affected by the changes in society and the forces which beset it.

In many respects the world has been in a state of revolution with the position of the individual at stake. Our own country, because of its democratic structure, has already made great progress in recognizing the position of the individual and in caring for his welfare.

In addition, it has been affected by the drive for individual recognition and achievement.

In the staff personnel area the individual has improved his situation by working with and through his peers in voluntary agencies. Frequently this leads to confrontation with other organizations and sometimes with the public in his total relationships.

Within this changing climate, new concepts of personnel administration have been, and are being developed as the concepts now in existence are beset by strong forces from employees, employers, and the public. It seems fairly certain that the nature of employee-employer relationship, now of such concern, will continue to dominate personnel policies and practices, though it is difficult to predict in any contemporary scene what aspect of the question will be foremost, since there is a continuing change.

The element of change makes all the more necessary the development of a body of democratic principles and a philosophical framework to guide personnel practice. Both principles and philosophy will be considered after we have noted the relationships of personnel administration to the changing needs of education itself.

Personnel administration and the educational program. The position, stated above, that the basic purpose of personnel administration is to facilitate the realization of educational objectives, leads to an examination of staff relations in the changing school system.

The size and anticipated growth of the educational enterprise suggests the proportions of the task in school personnel administration. In 1953–54 the public elementary and secondary enrollment was 28,000,000; in 1963–64 the enrollment was 40,217,000; by 1973–74 the estimated enrollment will be 46,300,000. Proportionate increase in staff has been experienced and will no doubt continue. In 1953–54 there were 1,037,000 classroom teachers in the public elementary and secondary schools; in 1963–64 the number had increased to 1,576,000; and the estimated number for 1973–74 is 1,916,000.[1] The management, deployment, and supervision in job assignments of this increasing body of organized and militant personnel is a task in itself.

Rising individual and professional ambitions in the growing staff

---

[1] Kenneth A. Simon and Marie C. Fullam, *Projections of Educational Staff to 1973–74*, 1964 Edition (Washington, D.C.: Office of Education, U.S. Department of Health, Education, and Welfare, 1964).

further add to the importance of the personnel function. It is not enough to satisfy the somewhat routine processes such as recruitment, assignment, and supervision; the morale and human relations aspects have taken an over-riding place in the personnel process.

One other change, the greater range in the character of the school population, is worth noting. Our dedication to meeting the needs of as nearly all of our youth as possible has led to a wide range of specialized personnel. The use of specialized personnel, and of the larger number of administrative and supervisory personnel resulting from the increase in the total personnel force, has led to problems of coordination that tax the most creative personnel leadership.

As each new task of the schools is undertaken—for example, the current emphasis on pre-school and adult education—a new dimension of personnel administration must be developed. The field of adult education is a first-class example of how this works out. Teachers of adults are frequently part-time, often high specialized personnel, who lack the dedication to the teaching profession found in the continuing full-time staff. The question of how personnel policies and practices should be related to this group and others like it places a new responsibility on personnel administration.

Philosophy and principles of personnel administration

Philosophy and personnel administration. The previous sections have emphasized the problems associated with the evolving nature of personnel administration. The personnel administrator must administer an effective and dynamic program that considers the human and morale factors of the staff as well as the educational objectives of the school system, and keep his sanity.

For such a task the personnel administrator requires a set of values implemented by guiding principles that will allow him both to maintain a safe and constructive course when beset by the forces around him, and to develop a new course when guidelines based on experience are lacking.

We call the set of values a philosophy. As it pertains to personnel administration this highly individual consideration must no doubt be based on a sound philosophy of education, a deep consideration for the human factor, and a thorough grounding in basic administrative practice—not only in personnel but more especially in general school administration and even in pertinent aspects of administration in other disciplines and fields of endeavor. The relative immaturity of personnel administration in education has left its philosophy only partially developed.

An illustration of the progress that has been made may be found in the Code of Ethics adopted by the National Education Association.[2] This code suggests that members subscribe to certain principles bearing upon their relationship to each other and to those whom they serve. Such self-imposed restraints evidence group maturity and are more frequently effective than a legal code. The dignity represented by these self-imposed controls is a tribute to the profession of teaching and greatly contributes to the integrity of the group.

The inter-relatedness of personnel administration with the activities of the profession itself, which has been referred to and which will continue to be stressed, suggests the philosophical direction that is being pursued.

Continuing attention to the development of a working philosophy will be related to portions of this text where it is appropriate.

Principles of personnel administration. Practically, behind the values are the guiding principles of personnel administration. The nature and number of principles that might be drawn depend on the detail with which the personnel worker or writer wishes to cover the field of his operation. Since it is impossible to cover all the situations that may arise it is better to consider only those principles that have relatively broad application and that can be understood by, and communicated widely in, the organization. One such principle of broad application is suggested as an example.

> Policy formation by the staff, subject to approval by the governing board, is a responsibility of the entire group, and those that are affected by a given policy should have a part in its development.[3]

The implications of such a principle are many and varied. It suggests a high level of democratic group activity and is based on confidence in the group's ability to determine what is best for it as well as for the children whose welfare is charged to it. It is likely to suc-

---

[2] National Education Association, *Implementing the Code of Ethics of the Education Profession and Strengthening Professional Rights* (Washington, D.C.: The Association, 1964), Appendix A.

[3] Harold E. Moore and Newell B. Walters, *Personnel Administration in Education* (New York: Harper & Row, Publishers, 1955), p. 19.

ceed with a professionally prepared group. It provides the high level of leadership required by releasing the creative talents of those in the group and of the leader. The authors from whom the single principle has been quoted have developed a number of principles, as have Van Zwoll[4] and Elsbree and Reutter.[5]

Each school system would do well to evolve, in a democratic fashion, its own guiding principles of personnel administration. These principles might very well become a part of board policy and thus provide a stable and continuing influence in the personnel practices of the district.

In subsequent sections of this book references, as examples, will be made to both philosophy and principles in the subjects under consideration. This will serve, it is believed, in putting the somewhat theoretical aspects of the discussion into a more practical framework.

Development of Personnel Administration

The process of personnel administration has always been present in the public school system. Whether directly performed by the board of education, as was the case in our early history when the board was the direct hiring, firing, and supervisory agent, or by the principal or superintendent along with their numerous other duties, or by a highly specialized administrative officer, the function has been present. As school districts have grown in size and complexity, and as professional education has obtained stature and specialization, personnel administration as a specialized function has taken an important place in the administrative process.

History of personnel administration. It is generally agreed that precedent for the position of public school personnel administrator was set in business, industry, and public personnel administration. Personnel administration as the term is commonly understood began with World War I. The recruiting, training, and paying of masses of workers in war production forced assignment of such responsibilities to specialized personnel.

The survey movement was largely responsible for bringing per-

---

[4] James A. Van Zwoll, *School Personnel Administration* (New York: Appleton-Century-Crofts, 1964).

[5] Willard S. Elsbree and E. Edmund Reutter, Jr., *et al., Principles of Staff Personnel Administration in Public Schools* (New York: Bureau of Publications, Teachers College, Columbia University, 1959).

sonnel specialization into school administration. School surveys conducted by management consultants, usually with a background in business, and by research and field study agencies in universities, particularly Teachers College, Columbia University, began, especially in the 1940's and later, to recommend the establishment of positions charged with the management of personnel.

The growth in pupil population in many school systems, forcing the employment of large numbers of teachers in the face of the short supply of qualified teachers, has led to the appointment of many directors of personnel in relatively small- and medium-sized school systems.

It is difficult to trace the history of the public school personnel administrator because frequently his duties as personnel officer were carried on under some other title, for example, assistant superintendent.

The first recorded public school personnel administrator was an assistant superintendent in Dallas, Texas, in 1919.[6] Detroit, Michigan, was also one of the early cities to establish a personnel administrative position. Now the position is generally found in medium to large school systems.

No exact count of the number of such positions is available but it can be safely estimated that there are about 250 such positions in public school systems. The three most common titles assigned to the position are director of personnel, assistant superintendent in charge of personnel, and administrative assistant for personnel. These officers are usually responsible to the superintendent of schools or, in very large systems, to a deputy or associate superintendent.

There is a growing body of research around the position of the personnel administrator. Doctoral studies and those by the Research Division of the National Education Association are especially helpful. The personnel administrators have a professional organization called the American Association of School Personnel Administrators[7] that is adding to their stature.

Definitions and scope of personnel administration. The nature of the function of personnel administration differs from system to

---

[6] National Education Association, Research Division, *The Public School Personnel Administrator,* Research Monograph 1962–M1 (Washington, D.C.: The Association, 1962), p. 23.

[7] The American Association of School Personnel Administrators is located in the Board of Education Building, Kansas City, Missouri.

system according to local policy. However, there is coming to be broad agreement in practice as to a working definition of the function. It is generally recognized as that complex of activities engaged in by the employing agency designed to secure employee effectiveness. Since what constitutes effective service is related to local objectives, the objectives of the employing agency are of considerable importance.

In education the tendency for the objectives of the employing agency and the goals of the employees to become more and more inter-related increases as teachers and other professional employees obtain a high degree of professionalism. This inter-relatedness colors the work of the personnel administrator in that it puts him close to a peer relationship with those he employs and supervises.

Another way to define the personnel activity is to set forth the elements in the process. In Chapters III and IV of this monograph the elements of recruitment, selection, orientation, assignment, promotion, transfer, separation, and retirement are listed and treated in some detail. In Chapter V important elements covering ethical, economic, and contractual relationships are discussed, and in Chapter VI such factors as morale, recognition, and appraisal are considered. Other publications in The Library of Education Series treat important aspects of the personnel process. They include staff welfare practices,[8] in-service education,[9] and the legal aspects of personnel.[10] All of these factors are a part of the personnel process and should be considered in trying to describe the function.

In defining the personnel function it is also important to recognize that it is a major and integral but not a separate function of the total school administrative process, which will be treated briefly in Chapter II. Also, one must distinguish between the personnel administrator and the personnel department, the latter involving the housing of the administrator and his aides, keeping records, and servicing the personnel.

---

[8] Leslie W. Kindred and Prince B. Woodward, *Staff Welfare Practices in the Public Schools* (New York: The Center for Applied Research in Education, Inc., 1963).

[9] John Clifton Moffit, *In-Service Education for Teachers* (New York: The Center for Applied Research in Education, Inc., 1963).

[10] Warren E. Gauerke, *School Law* (New York: The Center for Applied Research in Education, Inc., 1965).

Functions of Personnel Administration

Previous reference has been made to the relation of the objectives of the school system to the nature of personnel administration in the system. It is necessary to be more specific and also to set forth the objectives of personnel administration.

The personnel process. The previous section, and the later chapters, as well as the already mentioned books in The Library of Education Series make it unnecessary to treat the personnel process at great length in this introductory chapter. The purpose of referring to process at this time is to show that it involves the several elements in their relationship to the other functions of personnel administration discussed in the three following sections of Chapter I. The personnel process may well be regarded as the operating aspect of personnel administration, and the other three as providing purpose, stimulation, and service to the staff that is involved.

Development of personnel policies. One of the most difficult and challenging functions of personnel administration is to foster and develop policies that give direction and structure to the elements in the personnel process. The importance of involving the staff in the formulation of policies which affect the conditions under which they operate is well established and will receive further consideration in later chapters. At no place in the galaxy of duties of the personnel administrator are his qualities as a leader more tested when working with the staff, his fellow administrators, the board of education, and even the public, than in policy development. Policy gives both direction and security to the personnel process and, if developed through staff participation, provides an avenue for communication in the total organization. The responsibility for the development of personnel policy is one of the principal functions of the personnel administrator.

Morale and stimulation as functions. Assignment to a job in the system may be accomplished with great efficiency using appropriate methods of the personnel process, but unless the organization has a satisfactory level of morale and the staff has the stimulation or incentive to do a good job, only mediocre achievement will result.

Developing high morale and providing stimuli is one of the functions of the personnel administrator, although admittedly, many other people in the organization share the responsibility. The personnel administrator must constantly keep his finger on the morale pulse, alert other persons in the organization to conditions that influence morale, and take positive steps to improve it. The study of morale has become an integral part of the job of the personnel administrator, who has much interesting and pertinent research to aid him.

In somewhat the same manner he is constantly faced with the problem of stimulating the employees to bring about a higher level of accomplishment. In no other aspect of the personnel administrator's work is there a higher premium on creative administration. In carrying out this difficult function he usually must work indirectly, through other departments and staff, such as school principals, directors, and supervisors.

The growing activity of employee organizations gives him an opportunity to work directly with staff on matters very closely associated with stimulation and morale.

One of the problems the personnel administrator faces is to carry on this function along with the hiring, promotion, and dismissal aspects of the personnel process. Some school systems, sensing this problem, are separating the duties involved with the personnel process from those having to do with the broad aspects of human relations, including employee organization relationships, morale and stimulation, as well as some aspects of employee services. Whether this is a direction that will prove constructive cannot be ventured at this time. Currently, stimulation and morale relationships are important functions of personnel administration.

Staff services. A fourth most important function of personnel administration is to provide many services to the staff. Administering fringe benefits of all types and in-service education are two of the important ones. Since the personnel office holds most of the information about the staff, it also frequently aids other administrators, especially the superintendent and school principals.

In many systems the personnel office provides help for staff members who need educational and personal counseling. This latter function is especially important in a large and complex organization where stress, emotional problems, and complex human relationships are common. Both educational and personal counseling are associated with promotion and transfer of staff. Closely related is the matter of health service provided through physical examination pro-grams supervised by the personnel administrator.

These references to a variety of activities suggest that one of the most important functions of personnel administration is service to the staff. The quality of the service frequently affects morale in the staff and to a very large extent determines the image of personnel administration in the organization.

CHAPTER II

Organization and Functions of the Components of the School Personnel

The basic purpose of determining the organization and defining the function of personnel is that of facilitating the learning process within the framework of the objectives of the school system. There is no other justification for the hierarchy that is set up in the organizational structure.

Using this basic assumption the purpose of this chapter is to survey quickly the entire structural organization of the school personnel as related to basic educational objectives; to view briefly the duties and functions of the administrative and supervisory staff; to treat in greater detail the duties and functions of the teaching and the non-teaching staff; and to propose means of coordination of the entire school personnel.

Structural Organization of the School Personnel

In any discipline, one of the evidences of maturity is the development of a structural organization. At the same time this may become a problem since a fixed structure, lacking in flexibility and adaptability, tends to become an end in itself and not the means to, in the case of the educational organization, the achievement of educational objectives. While structure is necessary, this precaution is introduced at the outset to warn against becoming so involved with structure that educational objectives and human factors are lost in the desire to set up an "efficient" organization.

The school personnel structure functions, as was pointed out in Chapter I, within and as an integral part of the general administrative structure of the school organization.

General administrative structure. General school administration has been subjected to intense study and research during the past twenty years. Its relationship to public administration, business, and industrial administration has been explored. It is not our purpose to write extensively in this general administrative area. Another volume in The Library of Education by Jenson and Clark[1] has provided a panoramic view of the dynamics of educational administration and made excellent references to the changing scene in the administration of America's schools. Other writers, such as Griffiths,[2] have developed and described administrative theory and behavior. The administrative process in education has been treated by Campbell and Gregg[3] (eds.), and a recent volume of the National Society for the Study of Education also has dealt extensively with behavioral science as related to educational administration.[4]

While many variations and modifications have been suggested, no better school administrative organization for the local school district has been found than one wherein a single executive, the superintendent, is responsible to a lay board of education.

This position is supported by a recently issued statement of the Educational Policies Commission:

> The need to lodge final administrative authority in a single person remains as great as ever. But the importance of that person and of his work is increasing, for the development of knowledge and talents plays an ever larger role in the life of the nation. With each passing year it becomes more important that a community have competent educational leadership.[5]

Depending upon the size and complexity of the organization, the single executive should be supported and aided by assistants in specialized categories, including specialized help in personnel administration if the size of the organization justifies it.

In his work as the chief executive, the superintendent should be guided by a body of policy, approved by the board, which delineates his own duties, responsibilities, and qualifications, as well as those

---

[1] Theodore J. Jenson and David L. Clark, *Educational Administration* (New York: The Center for Applied Research in Education, Inc., 1959).

[2] Daniel E. Griffiths, *Administrative Theory* (New York: Appleton-Century-Crofts, Inc., 1959).

[3] Roald F. Campbell and Russell T. Gregg, eds., *Administrative Behavior in Education* (New York: Harper & Row, Publishers, 1957).

[4] National Society for the Study of Education, *Behavioral Science and Educational Administration*, 63rd Yearbook (Chicago: The University of Chicago Press, 1964).

[5] Educational Policies Commission, *The Unique Role of the Superintendent of Schools* (Washington, D.C.: The Commission, 1965), p. 15.

of his assistants. Such relationships are set forth in detail in materials directed toward the broad area of school administration. Jenson and Clark[6] have described organizational setting and structure at the local, intermediate, state, and federal levels; Moore and Walters[7] have related principles of personnel organization to the general administrative structure and have illustrated numerous patterns and theories of effective general administrative organization. They have also set forth the work and responsibility of administrative and supervisory personnel and have offered job descriptions of the principal administrative positions. In support of the necessity for a variety of administrative service, the Educational Policies Commission document previously referred to states:

> An adequate administrative staff also is necessary in any school system. Given the complexity of a modern school system, no man, except in the smallest district, can personally attend to all its administrative details. Nor can he have the knowledge in all areas that that administration requires. For these reasons, and because the superintendent needs time to exercise general direction and supervision of the school system, he must have the assistance of specialists of high competence.[8]

The increasing militancy of the staff further affects and perhaps complicates the role of the superintendent and his administrative assistants. The Educational Policies Commission document further notes:

> Teachers should play a major role in initiating and formulating administrative and policy decisions. In the interest of the advancement of education, the staff should seek such a role and the superintendent should welcome it. Most school policies and administrative plans are successful only insofar as they foster improved interaction between teacher and pupil, for classroom instruction is the most important function of the school. Policy making and administrative direction which ignore the professional knowledge of teachers and their knowledge of their specific situations are likely to result in poor policies and poor directives. Decisions should therefore reflect the pooled intelligence of the professional staff. In the interests of education this is a necessity, not a mere matter of professional courtesy.[9]

---

[6] Jenson and Clark, *op. cit.,* pp. 1–13.
[7] Moore and Walters, *Personnel Administration in Education,* Chapters 2 and 15.
[8] Educational Policies Commission, *The Unique Role of the Superintendent of Schools,* p. 19.
[9] *Ibid.,* p. 12.

The three quotes from the Educational Policies Commission document set forth the frame of reference in which school administration should be operating. The further discussion in this chapter bears upon the work and responsibility of each major employee group.

Duties and Functions of the Administrative and Supervisory Staff

Earlier statements have developed and amplified the idea that increasingly the administrative process in education is becoming one of democratic leadership where the chief administrator works with professional colleagues, each recognizing his own responsibility. Griffiths states that "All adminstration takes place within the context of organization."[10] In amplifying this position he states there are two types of organization, namely *formal* and *informal*. He describes each as follows:

> *Formal organization* is construed to mean an ensemble of individuals who perform distinct but interrelated and coordinated functions in order that one or more tasks can be completed. Thus, we have the business organization, the governmental bureau, the hospital, the public school. In each type of organization the task is more or less clearly understood by the general public. It is obvious that organizations result, in part at least, as a consequence of division of labor in society. It then follows that any *one* organization functions as part of a larger social system. The task of the organization must have value for the larger social system if that system is to tolerate the organization's development.
>
> An *informal organization* is present in every formal organization and is the system of interpersonal relations which forms to affect decisions made in the formal organization. This informal system is omitted from the formal scheme or is in opposition to it. The informal organization is a dynamic structure composed of special interest groups. In the past, the concept has been that of constant change—the informal structure being subject to continual revision as new decisions face the formal organizations.

While recognizing the existence of both types of organization, we shall be primarily concerned with describing the duties and functions of the formal organization.

How to effect the formal organization presents an interesting

---

[10] Griffiths, *Administrative Theory*, pp. 77, 80.

problem. An overview of the administrative process may help by suggesting what must take place within the structure. Many writers in education, business, and public administration have attempted to determine the essentials of the administrative process. *Administrative Behavior in Education,* a publication sponsored by the National Conference of Professors of Educational Administration, has brought much of the research together and has described the process in terms of the following seven components: *decision making, planning, organizing, communicating, influencing, coordinating,* and *evaluating.*[11]

It follows that the formal organization in the school system must provide for the performance of each component. There is still need to relate these components to the specific objectives that must be achieved and specific functions that must be performed. Herein lies the challenge: Who is to do what? Who is responsible to whom? How does one determine load? How can the day-to-day housekeeping tasks be kept from bogging down the organization? How can the organization be kept open-ended in order to have it remain creative? How are new tasks absorbed? Can it withstand crisis? Is it responsive to human factors? Does it follow principles of democratic action? Does it allow for individual initiative? These are a few questions that one faces in creating a *formal* organization.

Defining the functions and duties of personnel. Eight functions of the superintendency are graphically illustrated in the 30th Yearbook of the American Association of School Administrators. The representation shows the relationship between planning and evaluation and the ultimate organization of the school system. *Planning* and *evaluation* overlie the entire figure; *organization* provides a framework. *Personnel, business, buildings,* and *auxiliary services* establish the conditions which serve the educative process. *Information* and *advice* provide a two-way sharing of knowledge and ideas with the public and school staff. *Coordination* binds all together so that the personnel and materiel of the entire school system may be brought to bear on the major function of *instruction.*[12]

Having related the components of the administrative process and

---

[11] Campbell and Gregg, eds., *Administrative Behavior in Education,* pp. 269–317.

[12] American Association of School Administrators, *The American School Superintendency,* 30th Yearbook (Washington, D.C.: The Association, 1952), p. 81.

the function of the superintendent and his staff, the basis for the delegation of his responsibilities must be established. To a considerable degree this delegation depends on the size of the school district, but it also depends on the policies of the school board and on the objectives of administration. Usually delegation is related to specific functions, i.e., instruction, business, buildings, personnel, etc. The number of delegations directly responsible to the superintendent should be governed by an effective *span of control,* that is, the number of persons reporting to him. Opinions differ on what constitutes an optimum number, but a range of 3 to 5 is considered satisfactory, depending upon the range of the functions involved.

The chief administrator retains final authority, subject to the action of the board of education, although he may delegate important functions. If he follows a sound principle, the delegation of function must be accompanied by the necessary authority to perform it. Despite the importance and application of this principle, the chief administrator must be the one to answer to the board of education for the work of his assistants. This type of relationship is called the unit type of school organization.

Job classification and description.   It is not enough simply to make specific assignments and delegations; each needs to be classified and described if it is to be effective. School systems are increasingly classifying administrative positions and describing them in some detail in order to effect a more efficient administrative organization. Typical classifications include the title, assignment, and the basic responsibility, including to whom the position reports. In describing the job the duties are set forth, including the indication of the persons supervised. This type of specificity makes it possible for all concerned to understand exactly the extent and nature of the duties and responsibilities involved. It also should prevent staff members from confusing their duties and responsibilities with those of others.

If such a procedure is followed throughout the administrative structure, the possibly for a much smoother functioning organization is greatly increased.

In addition to job classification and description, school systems usually find it to their advantage to set forth their organizations diagrammatically. Line and staff charts are developed to show the relationships of the various positions and classes of employees. Such line and staff relationships have recently come under considerable fire. They have been described as inflexible, over-complicated, and confusing to employees who come into contact with more than one administrator in the hierarchy. Much of this misunderstanding can be eliminated if the human factors, including person-to-person relationships, sound policies, and good communication, are used.

Technique and structure of leadership. No amount of organizational structure will suffice unless, through inward convictions and motivations, those in the structure follow and practice democratic processes. Earlier emphasis was given to the leadership role in administration. Democratic leadership has many faces. It pertains to staff, board, and public relationships. The behavior of the administrator may not be the same in each instance. Only as a result of a philosophical orientation to the practice of democratic processes is he likely to follow them under the stress of operational problems. Perhaps the nature of leadership can be illustrated by the following quotation:

> The term leadership describes a relation between persons. It refers to interplay among persons. This relation results in one person having for a time the major responsibility for the activities and the welfare of the group. Leadership is displayed when one person affects another person or a group of persons in such a way that common direction is given to their efforts through this one person. Leadership is always accomplished in relation to others—never alone.[13]

Moore and Walters suggest the following further relationships related to democratic leadership:

> The goal of democratic leadership is not entirely altruistic. It is, of course, interested in the welfare of others and in the successful execution of a program that functions best when democratic procedures dominate its execution. It must be interested in such leadership because only through such processes can the leadership remain vital. No leader can expect to evolve for himself all the ideas he can fruitfully use. He needs the ideas of his group; and he needs, in active deliberation with his group, or selected representatives, to evolve new ideas.[14]

---

[13] Van Miller, ed., *Providing and Improving Administrative Leadership for America's Schools.* Fourth Report of the National Conference of Professors of Educational Administration (New York: Teachers College, Columbia University, 1951).

[14] Moore and Walters, *Personnel Administration in Education,* pp. 48–49.

In his function as a leader, as related to either his authority or the force of his personality, the school administrator may find himself operating in two roles—one which involves maintaining the established structure and another which initiates change in terms of the goals of the organization. Maintaining "the shop" is regarded as essentially administrative. Initiation of change requires a high degree of leadership. The distinction is not meant to indicate that either role is necessarily the more important; practice, timing, need, and relationship to the group must be taken into consideration.

The great challenge for the school administrator is to relate himself to the organization in such a manner that his goals and those of the group become so interrelated that a minimum of conflict results.

It is believed that the practice of democratic processes, especially staff participation in policy making and planning, which will have later emphasis, furnishes the key to effective leadership.

This position would indicate that the matter of leadership may be situational, that is, the "leader" may succeed better in one situation than in another, based on his relationships.

It also suggests that the school administrator may be more a "manager" of a situation than we like to admit. The leadership relationship therefore becomes "political" in character, using the term in its true meaning in contrast to its usual connotation.

Despite the multitude of studies[15] which have been concerned with the role of the superintendent and the leadership function, our knowledge of the area is still limited. One of the difficulties is that our judgment is frequently colored by the current scene. For example, at the present time the forces besetting public education in most communities force the superintendent in the direction of the "political" role referred to above. This is a departure from the *educational leadership* role that the profession has associated with the position. It is quite possible that in order to be an *educational leader,* proficiency as a *political leader* is necessary.

Duties and Functions of the Teaching Staff

Despite the fact that the teacher is the basic employee in the school system, and his service is at the heart of the objectives of

---

[15] National Society for the Study of Education, *Behavioral Science and Educational Administration,* Chapter VII, p. 142 ff.

the system, relatively little has been written with respect to his duties and functions. It is true that we say the principal duty of the teacher is to teach, but the broad implications of teaching have not been spelled out. Perhaps this is one of the principal reasons for the controversy concerning teacher education, the teacher's professional relationships, and his status in the community. This chapter will undertake to look at the duties and functions of the teacher, primarily the one working in the classroom, and to examine his community and professional relationships, since these have much to do with the personnel function.

The status of the teacher. There is much to indicate that our society is heavily oriented toward obtaining status. Therefore, the status of the teacher in society becomes an important issue since he operates at the heart of the school system. The teacher's drive to obtain status as an individual, and with relation to the organizations of which he is a part, provide many of the personnel problems and issues that will be considered in the subsequent chapters of this text. In examining the status of the teacher it is difficult to generalize since education in our country is highly decentralized and subject to a very large extent to local control.

The legal status of the teacher. It is generally agreed by authorities in the field of school law that the teacher is an employee of a school district and not a public officer.[16] In contrast, school board members are public officers and not employees. The distinction is legally important in terms of duties and rights afforded each group.

Despite the distinction noted and the general agreement by legal authorities, the public school teacher has certain characteristics similar to the public officer. "The position is created by the legislature; it is concerned with the public benefit; its powers and duties are fixed by law; the position rather than the person has permanency and continuity; it may require the taking of an oath; and the salary is fixed by law."[17]

The legal status of the teacher is further complicated by the fact that education, a state function, differs from state to state, although there are many common elements in the several state statutes. The usual basic legal qualifications for the teacher include certification,

---

[16] Madaline K. Remmlein, *School Law* (New York: McGraw-Hill Book Company, 1950), pp. 13–14.
[17] Warren E. Gauerke, *School Law*, p. 78.

citizenship, age, physical condition, character, and personal qualifications, regardless of the various state controls. With reference to certification, the courts have generally held that the teaching certificate is a license to follow a profession and it is to be regarded as a personal privilege, not a right.

Other common aspects of the teacher's legal situation include contracts, salaries, resignations, leaves, retirement, rights of appeal, and related areas.

A new factor has recently developed—collective action. Programs of negotiations and collective bargaining with school boards on the part of teacher organizations are opening a legal area new in education, although such relationships have long been familiar to business and industry as well as some classes of public employees. This development will receive further consideration in Chapter VII.

One other aspect of the teacher's legal status deserves mention in the limited treatment in this text. It involves pupil relationships. Two of the more common phases of this relationship that are dealt with by law are the control of pupils' conduct and the teacher's liability for pupil injury. In commenting upon the control of pupils, Remmlein states:

> Pupils have the responsibility of obeying the school laws and the rules and regulations of the state and local governing officials; they have the duty of submitting to the orders of their teachers and other school authorities. Failure to do so may result in corporal punishment, suspension, or expulsion. Corporal punishment usually falls within the scope of the teacher's authority; suspension and expulsion are usually within the discretionary powers of the school board. In the power to regulate pupils' conduct, the teacher stands *in loco parentis;* that is, the teacher is conditionally privileged to take disciplinary steps under certain circumstances and for certain purposes.[18]

The same author cites legal authority with respect to the position of the teacher concerning disciplinary action:

> As a general rule, a school teacher, to a limited extent at least, stands *in loco parentis* to pupils under his charge, and may exercise such powers of control, restraint, and correction over them as may be reasonably necessary to enable him properly to perform his duties as teacher and accomplish the purposes of education, subject to such limitations and prohibitions as may be defined by legislative enactment. . . . If nothing unreasonable is demanded, he has the

---

[18] Remmlein, *School Law,* p. 232.

right to direct how and when each pupil shall attend to his appropriate duties, and the manner in which a pupil shall demean himself.[19]

This short section on the legal status of the teacher has been limited primarily to matters pertaining to problems in personnel administration, and not meant to be a full consideration of the subject. Gauerke, Remmlein (to whom references have been made), Edwards[20] and others have written more extensively concerning this subject.

The job of the teacher. There are four basic relationships that are associated with the job of public school teaching. They are those with (1) children, (2) parents and citizens, (3) school board, administrative and supervisory staff, and (4) other school staff, especially peer relationships. These relationships are not isolated ones and despite the fact that the teacher-pupil relationship, as has been maintained, is at the heart of the teacher's job, the other relationships greatly affect the teaching of children.

During the past half century the shift in thinking concerning educational method has been from *techniques of presenting content* to *directing the learning of the child.* This emphasis determines in a broad sense the nature of the teacher's job. It suggests that there are four facets to his work, namely (1) teaching, or the instructional process, (2) the guidance function, (3) the school and community responsibility, and (4) participation in policy making and planning in the school system.

The teaching responsibility. This basic relationship, as previously noted, involves directing the learning of the child. It will vary depending upon the philosophy of the teachers and the school system. The public schools are undergoing serious criticism concerning the effectiveness of the teaching process, frequently because of misunderstanding or lack of compatibility between the school and the community with respect to philosophy and goals. This situation demands communication between the school and the community directed toward setting goals. Once goals have been established, the methodology of teaching is essentially a professional responsibility. The teacher should accept this responsibility since his preparation

---

[19] *Corpus Juris* (Brooklyn, N.Y.: The American Law Book Co., Vol. 56, 1932), p. 1088, as quoted by Madaline K. Remmlein in *School Law, loc. cit.,* p. 232.
[20] Newton Edwards, *The Courts and the Public Schools,* rev. ed. (Chicago: The University of Chicago Press, 1955).

has been directed toward academic and professional proficiency. He should also be able, with the cooperation of his peers, to interpret and defend his procedures. Within this frame of reference the teacher should enjoy and have protection of his freedom to teach.

The guidance function. Guidance, the teacher's ability to create a "climate" in which effective learning can take place, involves (1) understanding the process of human growth and development, (2) the psychology of behavior, (3) the mental health of pupils, (4) recognizing and meeting, frequently with the help of other professional personnel, the individual needs of pupils, and (5) the "teaming" with other professional personnel and laymen in using the total resources of the school and community to help the child. Guidance as defined above should be distinguished from the guidance and counseling service provided by persons especially trained in the field, now being incorporated into the program by many school systems, although the function of the classroom teacher is working with these specialists must not be overlooked. As the society becomes more and more complicated, causing emotional and mental health problems, the guidance aspect of the teacher's job becomes increasingly important.

The school and community relationship. This is directed to the basic citizenship of and the fact that every teacher is a teacher of citizenship. This relationship had greater emphasis when our society was more simple in its structure and when the teacher was generally known by the entire community. The citizenship aspect of the teacher's job cannot be separated from his adult citizenship. By carrying his proportion of citizenship responsibilities in the community and by being well informed and courageous enough to support a constructive point of view, he will demonstrate good citizenship as well as teach it.

Until all teachers recognize their citizenship responsibilities, both as teachers and as examples of citizenship and character, the effectiveness of the teaching profession will be less than it should be, and the degree of respect in which it is held by the public generally will be such as to reduce the public support of the profession and the schools.

This important area of the teacher's job may also be associated with his relationship to the parents of the children he teaches. Parent-teacher conferences furnish the teacher an opportunity to be seen as both a private citizen and as an educator. Seeing the teacher as a *person* is important and necessary; the effective teacher will seek individual as well as group opportunities to improve his image and thus extend his influence as a citizen *and* as a teacher.

Participation in policy making and planning. This is another important aspect of the teacher's job. In a sense this is his citizenship relationship in his profession and may involve him—directly or indirectly—and the school system that employs him in the state and national phases of education.

This important phase of teacher responsibility has numerous aspects. Too frequently it is considered as limited to his own school or school system. A more complete analysis of this responsibility includes promoting public understanding of education, helping develop local policies and programs, and influencing state and national educational policy.

In most of these concerns he will be working with his peers, especially through professional organizations. The relationships of professional organizations to school administration and to school boards is in a state of growth and change regarding policy and programs.

Professional organizations in the past have been concerned mainly with professional growth and welfare factors, and not with influencing, except indirectly, educational policy and programs. By adopting this latter role professional organizations in education have assumed a new dimension, one which comparable organizations in other fields, such as medicine and law, have practiced for some time. One of the characteristics of the maturity of an organization is its ability to act responsibly in times of stress. Organizations of the professional personnel in education are rapidly assuming stature which enables them to assume these new roles with dignity and effectiveness.

In discussing the trends in school personnel and its related problems in subsequent chapters, further reference will be made to collective action by teachers and its relationship to school personnel administration.

Summary. The administrator, and especially the personnel administrator, must be keenly aware of the many aspects of the teacher's job. Of all the sensitive areas of personnel administration, those matters that deal directly with the teacher's day-to-day work in the classroom and its corollary relationships, are the most sensitive.

The charge, all too frequently levied, that administration loses touch with the classroom teacher and the classroom relationship, should become a challenge to the personnel administrator. If a school system will recognize the importance of the work of the classroom teacher in several possible ways, the positive effect upon the morale of staff and the educational results obtained will be apparent.

Duties and Functions of the Nonteaching Staff

The function of the nonteaching personnel is, broadly stated, the performance of the services other than teaching, administration, and supervision that are necessary to the operation and maintenance of the school system. Terminology in this area is somewhat conflicting and this group of employees is frequently referred to as classified or non-certificated personnel. Numerous classifications of this employee group may be found but, if classified functionally, there are five types involved. They are: clerical, operational, maintenance, service, and a group that have certain professional qualifications but who do not teach or serve in an administrative or supervisory capacity. Within each type there may be, for practical convenience, several categories of employees. For example, within the maintenance group there would probably be carpenters, electricians, plumbers, etc. If each group were analyzed in this manner, there would be, depending upon the size of the system, from ten to fifteen to possibly a hundred different nonteaching jobs in the system. Since these jobs cut across numerous skills and services, the complexity of administering this group of personnel becomes apparent.

This area of personnel administration is further complicated by the fact that in nearly one half of the large school systems the nonteaching personnel are controlled by agencies other than the board of education. Local civil service, state law and city charter, and other special types of regulation affect their administration. In the limited space available only a few of the problems and issues that have been noted will be covered.

The job classification plan. The complexities of the administration of the nonteaching personnel require a system of job classification to bring order into a personnel field that has been characterized by considerable chaos. The principal uses of a job classification plan are that it (1) determines a uniform job terminology, (2) becomes a basis for recruiting and selecting new employees, (3) sets up promotion and transfer procedures, (4) functions in evaluation and in-service training programs, (5) becomes a basis for salary considerations, (6) contributes to good organization through a classification of relationships, (7) makes it possible to provide orderly accounting and budgeting, and (8) promotes good employee relations and efficiency, as well as lending dignity to this employee group.

The job classification plan is a *tool* in personnel administration. Its use by the personnel administrator gives promise of improving services in the nonteaching fields. Companion to a classification of the jobs is a description of each one of them. It is not enough to classify for example, the clerical services. Each must be described in terms of its title, function, qualifications required, examples of work involved, lines of promotion if any, salary range, in-service opportunities, and relationships to supervision.

While there are some general plans of job classifications for school systems, generally they must be developed locally because of the problem of adapting them to the size and needs of the school system, to local matters such as craft union relationships, and particularly to local pay scales for similar jobs in the community, especially in governmental organizations which require similar services.

Staff participation in developing job classifications and descriptions. It is possible to follow the principles of staff participation in developing job classifications and descriptions, thus developing higher morale and realizing the benefit from the potential of nonteaching staff. Too often personnel administrators overlook this valuable resource and underestimate the contribution that can come from the nonteaching staff. Since personnel administrators are usually drawn from the educational personnel, they frequently do not communicate well with nonteaching personnel.

The clerical staff. There is no rule of thumb, although there has been some research, relating the size of the clerical staff to the school enrollment. To a great extent the nature and size of the clerical staff is determined not only by the administrative requirements for clerical services but more especially by the extent of its use to free professional staff for more constructive service. New instructional programs, for example team teaching, are making greater use of clerical services.

The variation in providing clerical service between school systems, and even within school systems, suggests the need for a clearly defined policy and a job classification and description system that will provide for the variety of needs. Such a plan would permit specific job specialization, types of in-service training fitted to needs, an opportunity to fit salaries to responsibilities and competencies, provision for promotions, and, particularly, services fitted to the widely varying needs of the school system. Highly classified systems involving such considerations are more likely to be found where there are local or state civil service plans.

Selection and qualifications of clerical personnel. The employment of all personnel in the school system should be done with equal care. However, standards, skill tests, general education, successful work experience, and personal characteristics have not received as much attention in the selection of clerical personnel as in the professional field. This is an area of employment where the personnel administrator can have great influence since, to a considerable extent, the standards for employment and service are under his control. Clerical personnel employed by the school system should be carefully selected because of their relationship to children, the professional personnel, and the public.

In-service training for clerical personnel. Since the school is a teaching institution, it has both the opportunity and the know-how, if it will use it, to provide in-service training for its clerical personnel. Usually this in-service training involves merely the upgrading of skills, but it should also familiarize the personnel with systemwide relationships and practices that will improve efficiency and relieve professional personnel of detail work. In an organization of some size a skilled office manager who can judge work loads and efficiency, direct in-service training, write job descriptions, and organize work assignments can render a valuable service.

There is a growing movement to "professionalize" the clerical staff in the public schools. School secretaries have their own national organization, which frequently has local and state chapters, and which is taking the lead in "professionalizing" this area of service. This organization, called The National Association of School Secretaries—a National Education Association affiliate—holds state and national institutes, has developed a code of ethics, has professional standards, and publishes a magazine called *The Secretary*. Frequently, leadership from this organization can be used in developing local in-service programs.

The operational personnel. The operational personnel is that body of nonteaching employees whose responsibility is to keep the school plant and the auxiliary operating services, such as pupil transportation and delivery services, functioning so that the educational purpose of the schools may be achieved.

This is an extremely important service since the health, safety, and comfort of pupils and the educational staff are involved. This group of employees works with a large and valuable investment, which is increasingly becoming more complicated with highly developed mechanical systems involving heating, air-conditioning, and cleaning apparatus. The standards of housekeeping practiced by this group have a considerable effect on the children in the school and upon neighborhood or community conditions. In the area of pupil transportation the lives of over one-third of the nation's school children relate to services of school bus drivers.

Selection and qualifications, supervision, and in-service training of operational personnel. The earlier discussion with respect to job classification, job description, careful selection, and need for in-service training applies equally to this class of employees. If anything, an even more systematic policy and procedure should be followed with this group since they are less likely to have a formal background of education and training. In addition to the necessary skills to perform their tasks, these employees should be selected in terms of health, sobriety, vigor, morals, and ability to work with people.

The necessity for in-service training and supervision is especially important with operational employees. Except those coming from certain jobs in governmental organizations, few operational employees have the background or experience required for work in schools. Consequently, in-service training and supervision are needed. Some school systems, notably Denver, Colorado, and Minneapolis, Minnesota, have developed highly organized in-service programs that permit their employees to qualify for increasingly responsible jobs carrying higher pay and status. The responsibility for selection, determination of qualifications, and in-service programs is not entirely that of the personnel administrator, but he has a leadership and coordination role that is exceedingly important.

One of the special problems of the personnel administrator in the employment of operational employees is that some of the groups he uses may be unionized. In some states school boards are confronted by legal stipulations in dealing with unionized groups and the personnel director is forced to work within the legal structure.

Earlier reference has been made to supervising this group. The need for supervision and evaluation of these employees becomes apparent as one has experience in working with them. Usually they respond satisfactorily when supervisory methods are geared to helping them learn and progress in their job relationships. Associated with supervision is the problem of determining work loads. These should be geared to effective service as well as good employee relationships.

Another special problem in supervising operational employees, particularly building custodians, is the line of responsibility. The custodian should be responsible to the school principal in terms of the day-to-day operating problems in the school. The technical aspects of the custodian's work should be supervised by a technically qualified person who can advise and evaluate him with relation to his responsibilities such as cleaning, controlling mechanical systems, making repairs, etc. Again the best source of seeing these relationships is the well-prepared custodian job description which delineates those things that relate to his responsibility to the school principal and those that deal with his relationship to his technical supervisor.

The maintenance personnel. Much of the discussion pertaining to the operational personnel applies to the maintenance group. In fact, the personnel processes in many school systems are the same for both groups. The possibility of confusing the responsibility of operational and maintenance employees, if the school system is large enough to provide such specialization, is always present. Again, the importance of job classification and description must be stressed.

Maintenance workers, coming out of craft areas such as carpentry, plumbing, and electricity, are more likely to be unionized, with the resulting relationships that have been discussed. Frequently, too, these workers enjoy a higher pay scale than do many operating employees, and the nature of their work makes it possible to hold to a more exact day or work week. Such matters create for the personnel administrator potential morale problems. The wage problems for this group will be referred to in a subsequent chapter.

The service personnel. This growing group of employees in the public school system is essentially made up of cafeteria and lunchroom personnel. Some school systems also employ persons to help with traffic problems and teacher aides who work to relieve teachers of routine responsibilities. The bulk of the group, the lunchroom employees, constitute a special personnel program since much of the work is part-time and usually involves housewives whose background qualifies them for little other employment. Some of the jobs, such as managers of lunchrooms and head cooks, require more background and carry considerable responsibility. Job classification and description, related to duties and pay scales, are particularly important. There is a wide range of jobs of unskilled and semi-skilled nature in this group of employees and again in-service training is important. Supervision is also a major factor in managing them.

Because of the important relationship of the lunch service to the health of pupils, lunchroom employees are usually subject to special physical and medical examinations required by the board of health. This becomes a basic personnel requirement and relates, in addition to other requirements, to eligibility for employment.

Other nonteaching personnel. Within the school personnel organization, especially the larger ones, there are certain personnel from other professional or semi-professional fields and from certain skilled groups. Some of these are physicians, dentists, dental hygienists, nurses, recreation workers, architects, engineers, draftsmen, accountants, auditors, legal assistants, publicity and public relations assistants, and radio and television technicians.

While each professional or semi-professional employee renders an important service to education, he retains his own professional characteristics. This inter-relationship is necessary to the full performance of the services of the public schools, and yet a situation is created wherein the body of personnel practices built up by the school system to care for the majority of its employees do not fully or appropriately apply.

This is a special challenge to the personnel administrator since, in some instances, exceptions with respect to salary, working conditions, and general participation in the school system must be made. A careful definition of such services and their function in the school system, as well as encouragement and means for each professional group to respect the other, is important. Frequently this means that lines have to be established between professional organizations, and in some instances this is a challenge to the superintendent or personnel administrator since certain professional groups regulate, at least to a degree, professional practice.

Cooperation with such groups is important but the educator must not lose sight of his responsibility to the child.

The American Association of School Administrators, working with the American Medical Association, has developed in its *Health in the Schools*[21] a model for the relationships referred to above. This publication illustrates the painstaking care that is desirable in working out effective cooperation in professional relationships.

Coordination of the Personnel

This chapter has outlined the duties and functions of the three major groups of public school personnel. The wide variation in their functions and the specialized nature of their jobs creates a coordination problem that is experienced in few organizations. Specialization is greater as the public schools absorb the growing population, and the breadth of service to children increases. The problem is aggravated as the school administrator seeks talent from all professions and skills. The statement that the school employee group is diverse in skills and functions is by no means a criticism. The necessary services require this diversity. But the variety of service necessary in a school system serves to disunite the total employee group rather than to unite it. So the school administrator, with special emphasis on the responsibility of the personnel administrator, must find means to coordinate the total staff to the end that an adequate learning and environmental situation is created for the child. How to develop a "team" to accomplish this end is the special challenge to personnel administration.

Before discussing the problems and methods of coordination, the distinction between *organization* and *coordination* will be noted. *Organization* is, generally speaking, the arrangement of parts in a certain relationship to each other. In contrast *coordination* is a pro-

---

[21] American Association of School Administrators, *Health in the Schools,* rev. ed. (Washington, D.C.: The Association, 1951).

cess which results in those parts functioning in harmony with each other. The latter is the more difficult process and represents a challenge to the administrator, since it is through coordination of the several services and functions that the goal of achieving a good learning situation for boys and girls is realized.

Problems affecting coordination. The introduction to this section has suggested some basic problems related to coordination. With the risk of being negative, but at the same time looking at what must be overcome to accomplish coordination, the following problems have been noted.

The diversity of staff is the major problem. Only about two out of three are trained educational personnel, and even those have varied backgrounds. The one-third from outside educational preparation have had, as a rule, no special interest in, or background for, school work before they entered the employ of the school system.

School organization itself creates coordination problems. The vertical organization of schools, that is, by blocks of grades, and the horizontal organization into school units suggests the nature of this problem. A city with a hundred thousand school enrollment will probably have a hundred or more schools. In order to stimulate leadership, each school is given a degree of autonomy which may accentuate the coordination problem.

The fact that the personnel serving the schools is a body of public employees presents another factor affecting coordination. As public employees they are controlled, to a considerable degree, by state laws and local regulations; as individuals and members of a professional or vocational group, by voluntary controls of their professional, or other, relationships. This duality, although it may not in itself create a conflict, frequently creates a condition whereby coordination is made difficult.

Serving the public, especially working with children, is by no means the easiest of tasks, and this further complicates the problem.

Sometimes, too, economic and other factors disturb the employee group to a point where coordination problems result. The standard of living demanded by the public, particularly of its educational employees, is not always consistent with their means, and this is an added stress affecting coordination.

One of the characteristics of the personnel employed in the public schools is the high rate of turnover in the group. Turnover varies, of course, with the type of personnel being considered, and with the school district, and even with the state. However, this factor presents a special coordination problem with respect to the new groups of personnel that enter employment periodically.

Another factor affecting coordination is that a large per cent of the employed staff in school systems, especially men teachers with families, work at a second job both during the school year and in the summer. This problem in some districts is so serious that scheduling meetings of personnel outside of school hours is nearly impossible.

The application of uniform policies and practices in a school district is difficult because of the wide variety of employees. A certain uniformity is necessary if good results and morale are to be maintained. Too frequently the one-third of the employees who are not professional personnel are overlooked in policy making, particularly with relation to staff participation in this important activity.

A final problem relative to coordination is that of establishing administrative lines. Examination of the administrative structure of a typical school system reveals that many employees have dual and even triple relationships in the execution of their duties. The teacher works directly with the building principal, but also has certain staff relationships with area or subject supervisors or other specialists. The business and school plant administration programs are replete with problems which leave uncertainty as to lines and relationships.

This listing of problems of coordination is by no means a complete one, but it illustrates their nature. Means of effecting coordination are discussed in the following section.

Methods of coordination. The methods of coordination involve process, organization, communication and participation, principles and policy, personnel services, research and evaluation, and the necessary leadership to develop and obtain acceptance of common goals that will bind the organization together.

The factors that positively affect coordination are so inter-related that it is difficult to separate them for consideration. Their relationship cannot be fully developed in this limited treatment but separate consideration of these factors is done despite the risk that the reader will see them as entities. They may be likened to a fine musical instrument—not all of its potential is needed at any one time, but its full potential must be there in order to render the range of selections the artist performs.

Goals in the coordination process.   One of the most difficult but at the same time the most important means of binding an organization together and causing it to work in a given direction is through getting it to agree on and accept common goals. The primary function of the school administrator is developing goals and obtaining their acceptance. In this he functions at the highest leadership level. The methods of developing goals and the process of obtaining their acceptance cannot be developed at any length here. However, the acceptance by the group of as simple a goal as recognizing that the schools exist for the benefit of children in the society will provide a basis for overcoming factors and issues that deter coordinated action.

Principles and policy in the coordination process.   Earlier the relationship of principles and policy to the satisfactory operation of the school system has been noted. Staff relationships built on principles and policy have a firm foundation, since personnel can relate themselves to them and feel that all are similarly affected. Staff members react more constructively to principles and policy governing their actions than they do to rules and regulations, especially if they have been represented in their development.

Administrative relationships can be built on a positive basis when action is governed by well-considered and developed principles of operation and policies. It is recognized that every organization has to have a degree of discipline, the highest level of which is self-discipline. Understanding principles of operation and policies governing personnel provides at least a basis for self-discipline in the organization.

Organization and process as related to coordination.   Organization and process provide the skeletal structure in which coordination takes place. Considerable attention has already been given to organization, so only limited consideration is needed here. Coordination must have a vehicle in which to operate; within the organization there must be some understanding as to how things are done. An example would be decision making on some important issue. An understanding of the process involved leads to better acceptance of the decision and in turn less internal staff resistance. Coordination is made less difficult as internal resistance is reduced.

Communication and participation as devices for coordination.
The necessity for adequate communication in the staff and participation in critical areas of policy making and planning has already
been emphasized in this text. It is again noted to show its relationship
to the problem of coordination. The inter-relatedness of the methods of obtaining coordination can well be illustrated here by noting
that only through communication and participation can the system-
wide goals, the policies in effect or under consideration, and the
existing organization, as well as the process by which it was developed, be made known to the staff.

Personnel services and coordination. In Chapter I the functions
of personnel administration were discussed. The staff's image of personnel administration and the personnel administrator is largely the
result of the manner in which the functions are executed. The personnel administrator and his department should serve as a coordinating agency in matters pertaining to staff and should, through
policy development, services, communication, and organization,
make it easily possible for staff to turn to them for assistance when
problems develop related to coordination. If the "service" image has
been developed staff members will turn to the personnel department
without feeling that it is a threat to them, thus again strengthening
the self-discipline relationship which has been emphasized.

The personnel handbook and coordination. The importance of
the personnel handbook, essentially a personnel service, in the coordination process has been singled out for purposes of emphasis.
One of the most important personnel functions is the development
and periodic up-dating of a handbook summarizing goals, policy,
procedures, and conditions related to employment and service in the
school system.

Staehle in the U.S. Office of Education studied 72 administrative
handbooks for school staff personnel.[22] He found that the handbooks
all treated certain major topics although they varied in the degree of
emphasis on them. These topics are (1) school agencies and positions, (2) employment, (3) compensation and benefits, (4) employees' time, load, and absences, (5) personnel development, (6)
instructional programs, supplementary services, facilities and equip-

---

[22] John F. Staehle, *Characteristics of Administrative Handbooks for School Staff
Personnel,* Bulletin 1960, No. 13, Office of Education (Washington, D.C.: Superintendent of Document, U.S. Government Printing Office, 1960).

ment, (7) pupil personnel administration and services, and (8) community relations.

The importance of such information in the hands of all staff members cannot be overstated. However, effective administration cannot be achieved by mere conformity to regulations and perfunctory application of rules. Every employee must accept responsibility for the intelligent study and interpretation of general rules in relation to the educational needs in his own neighborhood, and must employ a judicious combination of wisdom and loyalty to school policies in the application of rules and regulations. It is to this end that the handbook should be directed.

One of the chief uses of the handbook as related to coordination is its value in orienting new members of the board of education and new staff members. Here continuity can be provided and better coordination obtained.

In some instances the handbook performs a legal function. State laws in some cases require that policies, as well as rules and regulations pertaining to staff and pupils, be published in some form and made readily available. Another legal function that the handbook performs is to define the pupil-teacher relationships as set down by state law and school board policy.

It is hard to see how good, as well as coordinated, operation can take place in a school system without a well-prepared personnel handbook.

Research and evaluation as coordinating activities. An important activity suggested earlier as a device for coordination is developing goals and objectives; the extent to which these are realized can be determined by research and evaluative procedures. Staff members need to know how effective the school system is and to what extent changes are necessary to achieve established or new goals. The basis and direction of change, quite a difficult process in a school system, can be established through research and evaluation. While not a specific function of personnel administration, research and evaluation, if viewed in their larger relationship to a school system, are aims of an effective personnel program.

CHAPTER III

Recruitment, Selection, and
Orientation of Staff

This chapter deals with the process of getting personnel into the classroom and oriented to their jobs. It involves two levels or types of recruitment—original recruitment into the teaching profession and specific recruitment processes with relation to certain jobs that may exist in a system of schools. Having recruited possible personnel for job openings, the selection process takes over. After the selection process has operated, the new staff must be oriented to the school system and to a given assignment. Seen as a continuum this cycle involves the profession at large, the individual, a teacher education institution, and a school system.

In this process the personnel administrator occupies a key role although his professional colleagues may be involved at various stages. In many respects the steps outlined are the most important aspect of the job of the personnel administrator since all that follows in the educational program is dependent upon what is fed into the staff.

Recruitment

The two aspects of recruitment referred to above will be developed in this section. The first is recruitment into the profession and the second is recruitment by the school system.

Recruitment into the profession. This relationship is a responsibility of the entire educational profession and broadly speaking of society, since the perpetuation of both depends upon having enough good teachers and other educational personnel. Because of the almost universal responsibility for recruitment into the profession, only limited consideration will be given to it here, with the work of the personnel administrator being emphasized. The size of this task is too frequently overlooked. There is a constant need for about 200,000 new teachers annually to care for the increase in pupil population as well as to offset the number who retire or leave the profession.[1]

The personnel administrator has two principal relationships to recruitment into the profession. The first is his particular responsibility as a professional person who should understand first hand the needs and requirements for educational personnel. In this relation he has a leadership responsibility among his colleagues, in the community, and as a specialist in the profession. He needs to be well versed in the profession and to be a protagonist for the profession. Unless he is a positive influence in his relationships to recruitment into the profession, it is unlikely that he will exercise his second most important responsibility successfully.

The second relationship is that of leading an organized program in the school system for recruitment into the profession. In this relationship his office should be a source of information with respect to supply and demand, certification requirements, and salaries. It should also be a resource center for others in the school system who deal with pupil guidance, public relations, and who are sponsors for organizations which work directly with recruitment, such as the Student National Education Association and Phi Delta Kappa. Some personnel offices provide simple publications on recruitment in general and recruitment for the school system that will give information to young people, parents, and prospective teachers who are interested in the school system.

Frequently system- and community-wide approaches are organized with committees made up of representative personnel and laymen being charged with recruitment responsibility. Usually the personnel administrator either is chairman of such a committee or serves it as secretary in order to give continuity and direction to its efforts.

Increasingly, recruitment into the profession is being recognized as a key not only to the quantitative, but more especially the qualitative aspects of securing adequate staff for the country's schools. Broader treatment of this subject, indicating its importance, has been provided by Moore and Walters,[2] Van Zwoll,[3] and by Lindsey

---

[1] American Educational Research Association, *Teacher Personnel,* Review of Educational Research, XXXIII No. 4, October 1963 (Washington, D.C.: The National Education Association, 1963), p. 355.

[2] Moore and Walters, *Personnel Administration in Education,* Chapter 8.

[3] Van Zwoll, *School Personnel Administration,* Chapter 4.

in *New Horizons for the Teaching Profession,*[4] reporting a project sponsored by the National Commission on Teacher Education and Professional Standards. The latter reference particularly stresses the teaching profession's responsibility, to which reference has been made, for replenishing and policing itself.

Recruitment for the school system. This is one of the specific jobs of the personnel administrator and usually occupies a large per cent of his time and energy. In this role he acts for the school system in trying to obtain staff that will fit its goals, program, and over-all needs. Some of his activities in this role pertain to the present, others to the future, and to a degree he looks back through the use of evaluative techniques to see if his role has been carried out successfully.

In looking ahead at the system-wide needs he must:

1. Plan and direct studies of present and future personnel needs;
2. Maintain close communication, in a line relationship, with other administrative personnel who supply information on long- and short-range personnel needs;
3. Assemble and coordinate information on personnel needs.[5]

In performing such tasks he will be guided by policy that is in existence and principles that have been developed. Where such guide lines do not exist he will of necessity try to have them established by the board, the administrative staff, or by representative professional groups, depending upon their nature.

An example of a policy is that only teachers with a bachelor's degree from an accredited teacher preparation institution will be employed. In trying to improve the quality of the staff, the personnel director may feel that an appropriate time has come for the policy to be modified to raise employment policy to the master's degree. He must gain professional acceptance, and administrative and board approval for the policy change before incorporating it into his employment policy. An application of *principle* to the change would be his use of the principle of staff participation in policy making and planning in effecting the policy change, as described in Chapter VIII.

Having determined personnel needs and having employment policies established to guide him, the personnel administrator will

---

[4] Margaret Lindsey, *New Horizons for the Teaching Profession* (Washington, D.C.: The National Education Association, 1961), Chapter 7.

[5] National Education Association, Research Division, *The Public School Personnel Administrator*, p. 41.

need to take another formal step. He will need fairly specific classifications and descriptions of the kinds of positions he has to fill. This
need is leading to a practice of developing job descriptions. In the
past such descriptions have been limited to the higher echelons of the
administration but are increasingly being used to cover a wide range
of positions in the school system. The function of the personnel
administrator in this relationship is to:

1. Study (or assist in the study of) and set up job classifications
2. Prepare specifications for the form, content, and administration of
job descriptions
3. Prepare or have prepared a description of a particular position by
a staff committee or by persons most closely associated with or who know
most about it
4. Maintain an up-to-date file of job descriptions
5. Be sure that specifications or descriptions include title, definition,
desirable qualifications, and typical duties and responsibilities
6. Study new or modified positions and alter the classification plan
as necessary.[6]

The step that logically follows in the process is an active effort to
secure staff for the position and for the district. Studies show this
occupies almost two-thirds of the time of the typical personnel administrator, and is regarded as possibly his most important function.
In this role, although he may not carry the entire responsibility, he
plans and carries out such activities as these:

1. Plans, directs, coordinates, and participates in the district recruitment program;
2. Travels to college campus placement offices to interest prospective
teachers in the district through talks, interviews, and participation in
career days;
3. Develops and maintains effective contact with college professors
and placement officers;
4. Encourages student teacher programs and related activities;
5. Advertises openings and prepares promotional brochures and literature.[7]

Because such activities are so important for the system, so expen-
sive and time consuming, an evaluation of recruitment activities is
important and necessary on an annual basis. Such evaluative reviews
should lead to a more efficient and effective operation, and are fre-

---

[6] *Ibid.*
[7] *Ibid.*, p. 42.

quently reported to the superintendent and the board of education, providing an opportunity for the review and modification of recruitment policies.

The recruitment program is one of the most important public relations activities in which the school system participates. It has public relations implications both for the school system and the community since the personnel employed become residents of the community at large. Although not frequently noted in his job description, the personnel administrator is, as a result of his recruitment activities, also a public relations emissary for his community.

Selection of Personnel

Selection is that aspect of the personnel process concerned with choosing persons with a high level of initial competency for the several jobs in the school system, to the end that a minimum amount of retraining and supervision is necessary. The initial selection from the recruitment reservoir after it has presumably been developed is also one of the most important jobs of the personnel administrator. Frequently, however, his colleagues play a larger role with him in this than they do in the recruitment process. Studies of selection processes indicate it is a cooperative relationship in most school systems, with line personnel reluctant to yield this responsibility to the personnel office. But despite the cooperative relationship the personnel administrator is usually a major influence in selection.

Role of the personnel administrator.   In general the role of the personnel administrator in the selection process involves (1) receiving and processing applications of prospective employees, (2) administering examinations if they are used, (3) preliminary screening of candidates' applications and establishing eligibility lists, (4) interviewing candidates in his office or in some other convenient location, as a college campus, (5) scheduling interviews for candidates with other district personnel, particularly line administrative staff who will later supervise them if they are employed, (6) assembling the results of all interviews and information on hand, reconciling differences in opinion if differences exist, and making recommendations to the superintendent and board for employment, and (7) issuing contracts to personnel whose employment has been approved.

In practice many variations of this role take place. For example, his authority may differ with classes and levels of employees. Usually he has greater authority in selecting elementary teachers than secondary ones since high school principals frequently exercise considerable control with respect to those selected for their faculties. Administrative personnel selection, too, is usually a primary responsibility of the superintendent or assistant superintendent for instruction. The selection of certain classes of nonteaching personnel is frequently almost entirely delegated to a line supervisor, an example being the selection of cafeteria cooks.

A well-organized personnel office should always be the repository of records on all personnel being considered for employment and the final recommendations for employment should be cleared through the personnel office.

Principles and policy as related to selection. In carrying out the role described above, the personnel administrator must be guided by a body of policy and by principles that will govern his action. Under the leadership of the superintendent, the personnel administrator, and other professional staff, the board of education should be encouraged to adopt policy that will clearly guide employment to the end that its further function will be to approve the recommendations of the superintendent and his assistants concerning personnel. Policy may concern itself with such factors as preparation, experience, eligibility for certification, personnel qualities, health, who is actually to do the selection or to participate in it, and the several steps that must be undergone before the individual is eligible for employment. These steps are usually a part of the recruitment and the selection process and typically are such activities as a formal written application, the interview, an observation of the individual at work if this is possible, evidence of a valid certificate, the use of tests or examinations in some instances, the filing of a signed oath of allegiance if required, and a formal acceptance of an offer of employment.

In addition to the policy relationship, it will be expected that certain principles will have been followed. If the system operates with job descriptions, it could well be an operating principle that the candidate's qualifications would have been checked against the job description that covers the position that is to be filled. Likewise the candidate should see the job description to know what is expected of him.

Operating relationships based on sound principles will lend confidence to administrative recommendations for appointments and develop an image with respect to the operation of the personnel office that will increase its stature with the staff, the board of education, and the community.

In recent years there has been a growing interest in personnel selection policies which stimulate professional performance in a school system. While such policies are broader than the selection area now under consideration, studies and statements on policy agree that (1) a policy, to be effective, should be a written, agreed-upon statement of directions for action, definite enough to be a guide, yet flexible enough to allow adjustment dictated by good judgment; (2) it should be formally adopted by the board of education and communicated to the staff and public; and (3) it is most effective if the group affected by it has had a part in its development.

Well-developed policies with regard to selection will go far to improve the quality of personnel selected as well as to guide and protect those responsible for selection of staff.

High priority problems related to selection. While there are many aspects of the selection process a few high priority ones have been selected for emphasis. They are the interview, examinations, recommendations, district requirements for eligibility, ethics in employment of staff, and contracts. Only brief reference will be made to some of these since further discussion will appear in subsequent chapters.

The interview. Nearly all school systems employ the interview as a technique of appraisal in the selection of personnel. The major purposes of interviews are to (1) appraise the candidate's personality generally, (2) inquire into the candidate's educational philosophy and educational outlook, (3) become acquainted with the candidate's ambitions and educational plans, (4) obtain further information, beyond the written date in the application form, on the candidate's education and experience, and (5) note first hand the candidate's physical characteristics, including his voice, manner of dress, and general culture.

Interviews may be non-directive or highly structured planned interviews, and may be person-to-person or on some kind of group basis.

The purpose of the interview in the selection process should govern its kind and nature. It should be a two-way communication relationship with each party giving and receiving pertinent information. The interview should be conducted in such a manner that both parties maintain their self-respect and professional outlook. These characteristics will require ample time and a comfortable situation in which to interview. The interview should leave each party with an understanding of just how he stands—that is, the employer should indicate if he expects to give further consideration to the candidate, and the candidate should make clear his interest or lack of interest in being considered further.

Probably too much dependence has been placed on relatively casual interviews in teacher employment. Interviews should be well planned, purposeful, and the interviewer should have practiced skill in conducting them. Also, too many employers of teachers develop the opinion that they have a "sixth sense" as related to interviewing candidates and depend too much upon the interview, when it should be regarded as only one aspect of the selection process.

Recommendations in teacher selections.   Written recommendations are still widely used in staff selection although their validity as a basis for appraising personnel being considered for employment has been shown to be in question. Unless the personnel administrator exercises care, he can be misled by them. Preparation institutions and persons writing recommendations differ widely, so comparisons of candidates are difficult. Generally those recommendations that come from personnel who have worked closely with teachers and from persons who supervise the prospective teacher in student-teaching are among the most valuable, and are ones upon which the employing official can place dependence.

The use of teacher examinations.   Only a relatively few systems use examinations as a device in selection, although several of the large systems that employ many teachers use them in certain aspects of the selection process. Some use examinations, either locally or externally prepared, as a screening device. The area of testing is broad and complex, and has not ben well developed as it relates to teacher selection. One exception is the National Teachers Examination, administered by the Educational Testing Service of Princeton, N.J., with results being made available to school systems. The values of this, or any other well-prepared, nationally used examination are

(1) that a common scale for evaluating professional preparation is provided, (2) that a good test will be so constructed as to permit comparison of standards from year to year, and (3) that better assignments can be made with the information coming from the examination.

Opinions differ widely on the use of examinations and school systems should enter upon their use only after careful appraisal of the examination as related to the function it is expected to serve.

District requirements for eligibility. Formerly school districts had many requirements related to appointments such as local residence, marital status, religious and racial discriminations. These are generally being eliminated as they adversely affect employment in terms of securing the best person for the job. Professional organizations have stressed the elimination of such requirements and, as provincialism generally has tended to dominate our society less, they have been removed. But there are still "unwritten" requirements in many communities which adversely affect getting the best personnel for the schools as well as providing them the freedom to teach and learn.

Employment ethics and contracts. These topics are referred to here only to relate them to the context of selection practices. They will be treated in Chapter V.

Summary. This entire discussion has been directed primarily toward the selection of the professional staff. The organization, policies and principles that have been discussed are generally applicable to the nonteaching personnel as well. The personnel administrator will need to make adaptations to this classification of personnel such as those suggested in Chapter II. Usually nonteaching personnel are recruited and selected from the community in contrast to the wider area from which the professional staff is drawn. This may affect employment practices, in some cases complicating them.

The problems in the selection of teachers and other staff members, like many other problems in school administration, require professional stamina and fortitude on the part of the superintendent of schools and the personnel administrator. The educational welfare of the children in the school should be the first consideration. Their interests demand that appointments follow the basic principle of selecting the best person for the given position that the available salary will attract.

Orientation and Induction of Staff

The orientation process involves familiarizing the new employee with the various aspects of the school employment for which he has been engaged, and with their implications for him. Determining what shall take place in the orientation program and who will be responsible for carrying it out is an organizational task within the school administration. Staff participation in developing orientation programs is recognized as sound, since who will know the problems in starting to work in a new school and community better than persons who have recently experienced this induction?

Purpose of orientation. It should be the mutual concern of the school administration, the professional staff, and those newly appointed to work out means by which the new staff is quickly absorbed into its new responsibilities. It is generally recognized that despite the sound professional preparation of new staff, there are many frustrating and difficult problems in getting off to a good start in a new school situation. It is the purpose of orientation programs to anticipate as many of the problems as possible, and, by providing help in solving them, to get the instructional program under way with the least friction. A look at orientation programs in good school systems yields certain information with respect to their character. Some of the principal areas covered in orientation programs are (1) a welcome to the professional group, including professional associations, (2) becoming acquainted with the school building (and its program) where the teacher is to work, (3) learning about school regulations, concerning payroll procedures, absences, substitute teachers, the school day and calendar, textbook and library practices, etc., (4) learning about the community, such as churches, banks and financial institutions, housing, credit, newspapers, parent and teacher organizations, etc., and (5) being furnished with the personnel handbook, codes of ethics, board rules and regulations, parking permits, insurance programs, etc.

One of the most important services is providing a way for new people to get their questions answered without embarrassment. Some school systems associate new personnel with experienced personnel in a "buddy" system to accomplish this.

Having looked at the purposes of orientation programs and some of their components, it remains to discuss the responsibility for blocks of the program.

The personnel administrator and orientation. Earlier it was noted that the personnel administrator usually functions on a district-wide basis. Some of the activities involved include furnishing and interpreting district regulations, policies, and school district and community services to the new employee. As part of the orientation activities, frequently the personnel records of new employees are completed. It is within this series of activities, coupled with his earlier contacts with the personnel office during his application and employment, that the new employee obtains his image of personnel services in the district.

The school principal and orientation. It has been indicated that much of the induction process goes on in the school to which the new employee is assigned. The principal and the professional staff must acquaint the new staff members with the school and its program. Many of the questions about such matters as absences, substitute teachers, the school day and calendar, textbook and library services, payroll regulations, insurance programs, and the like can best be answered in the smaller groups that school meetings afford. Above all, a rapport should be developed in this smaller group that will permit the new employee to feel that he "belongs," that his success is important to the principal and the remainder of the staff, and that he matters as an individual.

The professional staff and orientation. Increasingly the professional organizations are assuming some responsibility in the orientation process. There are many things the professional organizations can do better than the school administration, such as encouraging membership in professional organizations, urging participation in in-service activities, providing some social activities, relating the new employees to community relationships, helping with housing problems, stressing the importance of codes of ethics, etc. Imaginative professional leadership will find many ways to help the new staff and, in the process, will build a healthy respect for the profession.

The community and orientation. The community that overlooks its opportunity to fit into the orientation program is failing to render a service that will repay it great dividends. Making the new employees welcome and a part of the community life is important even from a dollars-and-cents standpoint. The community, through school district taxes, has already invested several hundred dollars in the new employee through recruitment and personnel services expense. To help make him a satisfied and effective employee who will remain in the school system and community life should therefore be a *community* objective. Given the opportunity by the personnel administrator, many communities will do a fine job. In some communities men or women's clubs, the PTA, churches, and other groups have taken the initiative. Sometimes newspapers, radio, and television stations assist. The potential in community relationship to orientation of new staff is scarcely touched.

Making orientation a continuing process. Many school districts organize their orientation activities on a week-long basis just before school opens and make these days part of the contractual period. Included are many of the activities to which we have referred and others more specifically oriented to the educational program. These latter activities may well be related to other in-service training throughout the year. Having a meaningful continuum of activities adds both to the original orientation activities and the later in-service program. Frequently the orientation period can be used to probe needs and interests and plan the continuing activities. The way creative and imaginative school leaders and their personnel can work together is well illustrated in *In-Service Education for Teachers,*[8] to which we have already referred.

Among the important suggestions by Moffitt is that orientation, staff improvement, and evaluation are a continuum and that they should be seen as such. If this approach is attempted, staff participation in policy making and planning with respect to these activities is of great importance. Without such participation very little can be accomplished.

---

[8] Moffitt, *In-Service Education for Teachers,* Chapters 1, 2, 5, 7.

CHAPTER IV

Assignment, Transfer, Promotion, and Separation of Staff

The previous chapter dealt with the process up to the point where the new employee has been oriented to the school system and possibly assigned to a school which may also participate in his orientation. This chapter continues the discussion of the personnel activity through which a staff member passes, beginning with recruitment and ending with separation through resignation, dismissal, or retirement.

Assignment

Assignment as treated in this chapter deals with the broader problems of relating the competency of the new employee to a specific job.

When a teacher signs a contract with a school district, he may or may not have agreed to teach a specific grade or subject. Especially if the school system is a large one, his contract will be in such general terms as "to teach in the elementary grades" or "in the secondary schools" in contrast to a specific grade or subject in a particular school. In fact, some contracts are even more general and indicate that the individual is to "teach" in the school system, subject to the laws of the state and the policies of the local board of education. This leaves the specific assignment up to the superintendent, the personnel director, and others who share the professional responsibility.

The necessity for such a general approach may be understood when it is realized that some school districts hire several thousand new teachers each year, beginning in February and March, against needs that may not be determined finally until August.

Such a situation presents a problem as well as an opportunity and it is to this situation that this section is devoted.

Factors governing assignment. The interests of the school dis-

48

trict in the welfare of pupils as well as of the teacher must be considered in this phase of the personnel activity. Certification requirements and the standards of accreditation agencies offer some protection against unreasonable and unsound practices in assignments. However, these serve only as general guides and a more studied procedure that will relate individual competency to a specific school need should be the goal of the personnel officer working closely with those in charge of instruction and, more especially, the principal of each school.

The responsibility of the principal, operating within the framework of general school policy, to delineate the specific job needs in his school cannot be overstated. If he prepares sound statements of needs, realizing that certain flexibility must be maintained in order to relate them to the potential supply of teachers, he will improve the possibility of the assignment of a satisfactory staff to his school. Unreasonable and unsound combinations of subjects, extra-curricular assignments, or personal requirements will render the ultimate assignment less effective.

The relationship between selection and assignment becomes apparent as one views the continuum. The process of assignment is so involved that in our limited treatment of the subject we can do little more than to indicate basic philosophy, principles, and factors affecting assignment. So far in the discussion a point of view has been developed. Some principles that should govern assignment are: (1) it should be related to the basic preparation and professional interests of the teacher; (2) the previous educational, and other, experience of the teacher should be considered in the light of the make-up of the faculty to which he is being assigned; (3) the immediate and long-range specific needs of the school should have primary consideration; (4) the personal interests of the teacher, as far as they can be considered, should be honored; (5) the job assignments should offer reasonable opportunities for success and ultimate promotion; (6) the goal of developing the total strength of a school faculty must receive consideration; (7) the nature of the neighborhood in which the school is located should be considered; and (8) the legal and accreditation requirements should be met.

The importance of following such principles and considering the factors related to them in the assignment of the beginning teacher should be given particular consideration. The problems of adjustment to a new situation are serious in themselves and, if coupled with a poor assignment, may make success in the first year of teaching virtually impossible.

It should be recognized that perfection is never obtained in a large organization. The continuing nature of the problem suggests the importance of a personnel practice that permits identification of unsatisfactory or undesirable assignments at the outset and makes provision for help to the persons involved. Load modification, in-service assistance, and recognition in the final evaluations of service are a few considerations that may help.

One of the measures of success of personnel administration is the degree to which harmonious assignments, considering the welfare of children in the school system and the professional and personal interests of staff, can be achieved.

Unsatisfactory assignments may be a principal source of morale problems as well as of instructional inefficiency. Outright mistakes, such as secondary teachers being assigned to primary teaching or secondary teaching assignments outside of major or minor subject matter preparation, frequently become public relations as well as professional issues.

Load as a factor in assignment. Determining a fair and productive load is one of the most difficult personnel responsibilities and is a continuing problem throughout the professional experience of the, teacher. The load factor also relates to personnel problems such as morale, additional pay for overload or extra duties, the health of the staff, and quite frequently to staff turn-over.

Almost every study of working conditions for school staff refers in some way to the problem of load. Such studies show that the load is composed of (1) the actual classes or grades taught, (2) operational activities such as committee assignments, reporting pupil attendance, teachers' meetings, and administrative assignments, and (3) extracurricular duties, frequently after school and not directly associated with the teaching job.

Other intangible factors are related to load. If the work to be done occurs under favorable conditions the outlook of staff with respect to load may be very different from one in which the climate is one of tension and general unrest. Even appreciation or lack of appreciation may affect staff feeling with respect to load. Whether an overload is temporary or permanent also may be a factor in staff reaction.

Lately there has been considerable effort on the part of school administrators and teachers, under the leadership of teacher organizations, to free the teacher to carry out his primary responsibility of teaching. One of the principal studies, "Time to Teach," sponsored by the Classroom Teachers Organization of the National Education Association has this to say about the problem:

> Careful analysis of the teachers' classroom problems, information on which has been gathered from all parts of the country, suggests three vital fronts on which the time to teach battle must be waged.
> The first front, conditions of work, deals with the policies established by the school board and administration with respect to the responsibilities of teachers. The differences in these policies across the country are enormous, and, in some instances, policies are such as to have a debilitating effect on teacher efficiency. A school system which fails to provide its teachers with an opportunity to eat lunch in a quiet room, free of stress; which allows unnecessary class interruptions; and which burdens the teacher with many nonprofessional tasks fails to understand the nature of teaching and the limits of human endurance.[1]

The basic question is whether loads can really be equalized and, if they cannot, whether pay schedules reflect an equitable recognition of the variations in load. This question will receive fuller consideration in Chapter V. Some students of this problem have hypothesized that the differences in the capacities of the staff members themselves make it undesirable to try to equate load through a formula or other means. It is a well-known fact that some staff members voluntarily take on and even seek extra assignments because of their initiative and professional interest.

Definitive studies are needed in several areas related to the problem of load. All too little is known on the basic question of the relation of class size to load.

Another factor frequently not controlled by school policy is the outside work load of the staff. Some studies show that a large per cent of teachers, particularly men, hold jobs outside the school system. Many women teachers are also homemakers and carry a heavy work load in their homes. How to relate this problem to the complicated one already discussed, concerning work load in the school, is at this time unsolved.

---

[1] Malcolm M. Powers, Director, "Time to Teach Project," *National Education Association Journal* 54: 17–18, May 1964.

Length of day and year related to load.   Currently the demands in the educational program are causing many educators to consider lengthening the school day and the school year. What constitutes the optimum length of these is an unsolved problem. Should either be lengthened appreciably there would be immediate questions concerning such action as related to the problem of staff load. This is a highly complicated problem and relates to the students, their parents, and the staff. Changes are inevitable as society places heavier and heavier loads on the schools.

Well-defined policy needed.   The foregoing discussion on load suggests the need in every school system for well-defined policy arrived at by the board of education with extensive community and staff participation in its development. Such policy must have as its center of interest the welfare of children and youth.

Transfer and Promotion

The close relationship of transfer and promotion in the personnel process has led to their association in this text. Both activities are related to the work of staff after the initial assignments. Both activities are also highly related to the morale and well-being of the staff and the school system.

It is not always possible initially to assign staff in situations they and the personnel administration will consider optimum ones. Therefore, carefully developed policies and procedures relating to transfer and promotion of staff play an important part in over-all personnel policies and procedures of good school systems.

Transfer policies and procedures.   Relocation of staff personnel may become necessary to meet load conditions, instructional requirements, and for other good reasons including the wishes of employees for opportunities of service elsewhere in the system.

It should be the responsibility of the superintendent, working through the personnel director and the affected principals, to effect transfers, hopefully with full cooperation of all the parties. However, the superintendent should have the authority, subject to board of education review, to make transfers for the good of the school system. No transfer, however, should be made arbitrarily or vindictively. Causes for transfer should be reasonable, and understood by those concerned.

Applications for transfer should follow a procedure established through staff participation in policy making and be fully understood by the total staff. Staff members, both those in administration and teaching, should follow the time schedule established in written policy for making or requesting transfers.

Instructional needs, qualifications, loads, and seniority, all other things being equal, should provide criteria for decision making on transfer requests.

From such reasoning as outlined above, policies could be established and procedures evolved. Such policies and procedures should be in writing and subject to periodic revision, again in a participatory process.

Quite often in a growing school system persons are employed with the understanding that they will be moved later to another assignment. An example is that a secondary teacher might accept employment as a junior high school teacher with the understanding that he will be transferred to a senior high school when there is a position available in his field. Such cases should, while subject to the usual transfer policies and procedures, be made a matter of record so that later misunderstandings will be avoided.

One of the vicious personnel practices that has developed in some large school systems is that of transferring an unsatisfactory employee instead of facing up to his unsatisfactory service record. As in the case of selection and assignment, the transfer of a staff member should be related to the interests of the school system. Earlier statements suggested that the morale and well-being of the employee should be considered, but it must be remembered, when an extreme problem of poor service is involved, that the rights of the children supersede those of the staff member.

Promotion policies and procedures. This area, like transfer of staff, is a delicate one since it affects morale and involves the human relationships of the individual and associates.

The conditions in a system that make promotions possible are new positions resulting from growth, new job classifications, and vacancies caused by death, retirement, transfers, and demotions. For the most part "promotions" in a school system require the individual to leave the classroom, either part or full-time, and this in itself raises the question as to what is the highest function in a school system. Certain positions are sought through promotion largely because they are higher salaried than classroom teaching. It should be made clear that not all employees, especially teachers, seek promotion. Many teachers enter the classroom because of their interest in and love for teaching and do not want to be promoted into an administrative or other position. In fact, many teachers refuse offers for other than classroom teaching assignments. As a result we are dealing with a limited but aggressive group in those who are seeking promotions. Because this represents an internal pressure situation, it often causes problems in administering personnel policy in this area.

A systematic promotion policy establishes bases for advancing personnel from within the organization and makes provision for such promotions to take place by way of procedures set up to make them defensively possible. Such a plan creates at least the bases for a career situation for employees. The most important contribution of a systematic procedure is to prevent capricious action from either the administration or the board of education which would undermine the morale of the staff. Thus, in the long run, systematic procedure relates to the recruiting potential and holding power of the system.

Since there are more administrative positions, particularly principalships, than any others to which staff may aspire through promotion, more study and research has occurred in this area. Such study and research has been chiefly in large school systems and in colleges and universities, or in a combination of the two. Tests, observed internships, batteries of interviews, in-service activities, and preparation programs involving higher degrees have been used to screen and determine those eligible for promotion.

One activity normally associated with a sound personnel program is the periodic appraisal of the employee's service. Records of such appraisals are also an important factor in screening for promotion and should be related to the expressed desire on the part of the employee for promotion to a given position. Usually promotional opportunities come after the candidate has served a probationary employment which makes a period of observation and appraisal possible. The early identification of those potentially qualified for promotion should be a part of any well-organized procedure on promotion.

In school systems where several positions of the same type may develop over a short period of time, in-service orientation courses have been organized and opened to those seeking, or invited to seek, promotion. The elementary principalship and the assistant principalship of the secondary school are two of this type most frequently found.

While the weight of the argument is in favor of promoting from within, if there is qualified personnel, there is another side to the question. It can result in too much "in-breeding" so far as ideas and practices are concerned. Resentment on the part of staff not promoted and charges of favoritism often offset the good expected from promotion from within. The size of the school system, as well as its resources for in-service activities, often affect promotion policies.

A recommended practice of posting notice of vacancies in the system is important, since personnel frequently would like the opportunity, even if they do not avail themselves of it, to consider applying for openings.

Whatever the final policy of a school system may be on promotion from within or without, nothing should get in the way of the more basic one of selecting and promoting based on excellence and competency.

Separation Policies and Procedures

Permanent separation from the staff of a school system involves dismissal, resignation, or retirement. Temporary separation may involve suspension and leave, either voluntary or enforced. These relationships are usually covered by state law and consequently take on a somewhat different character from many of the other personnel activities discussed in Chapters III and IV. In school systems with good personnel policies, the legal relationships are usually augmented by local board policies and procedures. Frequently such policies and procedures differ as they apply to probationary or tenure teachers and to administrators under contract. Consequently there may be a wide difference between states and even school systems within states with respect to the legal and policy relationships concerning separation. Because of that difference this text can deal only with the problem on a general policy and procedure basis and urge the reader to familiarize himself with his state law and the procedures of local and, in some cases, state boards of education.

Permanent separation of staff.   There has been little treatment in the literature on personnel of this aspect of the personnel activity. At least two of the categories of separation that are being discussed are negative in character, and retirement is usually an unpopular subject, too. However, there is real need to examine policy and procedure with respect to the three areas referred to in the introduction.

Dismissal of staff. Dismissal of staff as provided by law must be for cause. Causes prescribed by law usually include incompetency, neglect of duty, immorality, insubordination, justifiable decrease in number of teaching positions, or "other good and just cause." The teacher under a probationary or tenure contract would be subject to action within this framework of causes. The probationary teacher whose contract has expired would have no status in such action. State laws usually prescribe a procedure as well as cause. Procedures commonly cover a written notice, a waiting period during which the teacher can ask for a hearing, a written statement of reasons for the dismissal action, the right to be represented by counsel, and frequently the right to appeal to the courts, especially if a procedural violation has occurred.

Boards of education are thus free of legal technicalities and may either indicate in their policy statements that their dismissal policies coincide with the state law or ignore a policy statement in this area since they would be under state law anyway.

More and more teachers suffering dismissal action, especially if there is some professional issue involved, have the benefit of the assistance of the legal section of their professional organization or union. With such support relatively few dismissal actions take place. The activities of the National Commission on Professional Rights and Responsibilities of the National Education Association have protected many teachers from unwarranted dismissal and clarified the legal status of teachers. Grievance committees of teacher unions have also defended their members.

Resignation of staff. Most resignations of staff are voluntary and occur for good and just reasons involving personal and professional causes. The greatest number of resignations of women are for marriage or maternity. Both men and women resign to take other positions in the profession or more lucrative jobs outside the profession.

State law and school board policies usually prescribe notification procedures with respect to resignation under penalty of revocation of teaching certificate or financial penalty. These are seldom enforced since professional ethics provide an even stronger control than such penalties.

Resignations are also involuntary and are sometimes demanded where the teacher's service is unsatisfactory but where there is reluctance to go through a dismissal action because of the publicity adverse to the teacher and the school system. While infrequently used, this procedure is sometimes abused and teachers are forced to resign rather than become involved with a dismissal procedure. Professional ethics again are a factor in such relationships and, fortunately, most educators in personnel positions do not abuse their authority to secure involuntary resignations without cause.

Research is needed on the *real* cause for the numerous staff resignations. It is generally known that the stated reasons are not always the real reasons. Many personnel administrators are using an "exit" interview procedure in order to determine the real cause for resignations in their school systems. The results of such interviews provide a basis for modification of personnel policy, correction of conditions in certain schools, and improvement of working conditions.

Professional associations are also cooperating in such studies since they have membership and status at stake. It is believed that through the cooperative efforts of personnel officers and professional associations greater stability can be effected in school staffs.

Retirement. The discussion of retirement in this text refers to it only as a personnel activity and not in a staff-welfare relationship. The latter is treated in another volume of The Library of Education.[2]

Retiring from service is a difficult transition for most individuals. Bridging the gap smoothly from an active to an inactive status requires more than the assurance of financial security.

It is a personnel responsibility to help prepare staff for retirement. Many school systems are providing gradual retirement by giving opportunities for the continuation of limited service and are continuing certain benefits, such as insurance programs, social opportunities, and group housing services. Continuing participation in cultural opportunities involving the active staff, and even being kept on mailing lists for school information reduces the psychological impact of retirement.

Policy of this sort contributes substantially to maintaining the

---

[2] Kindred and Woodard, *Staff Welfare Practices in the Public Schools, loc. cit.*

morale of retired employees and enables the school system to continue to capitalize on the special talents and resources of the retired staff.

The variety in retirement programs so far as age and benefits are concerned suggests that each school system develop appropriate policy and procedures of its own. The frequent combination of local and state retirement plans with the social security system requires that the personnel administrator be familiar with each system and that the program of information to staff include facts concerning them. By enlisting the cooperation of local and state professional organizations, the personnel administrator can obtain assistance in preparing staff for retirement and providing continuing service to retired staff.

Usually retirement plans cover the nonteaching staff also. This group must not be overlooked in information and service programs.

Studies have shown that the retired school staff, like that in business, industry, and government, can benefit from a counseling service in three areas—financial, physical, and emotional.

Temporary separation of staff. Previous reference has been made to the temporary separation of staff involving suspension and leaves. A brief discussion of the first and a treatment of the second as a personnel activity will follow. Leaves such as professional leaves, sick leaves, etc., are treated extensively in *Staff Welfare Practices in the Public Schools* by Kindred and Woodard, another volume in The Library of Education Series.

Suspension of staff. A suspension is a temporary deprivation of the staff member's rights and privileges. Such action is usually taken pending an investigation which may or may not lead, depending upon the findings, to a dismissal action. Frequently, suspension is used to get a staff member out of contact with children or other staff members for the welfare of the school. Suspensions are usually governed by law or policy or both and frequently are executive actions subject to board review. This type of personnel action is rarely used but must be within the authority of the personnel administrator if the welfare of children has first consideration.

Suspensions not punitive in nature are occasionally used when there are more staff members than necessary. Whether such action is legal would depend upon tenure and contract rights.

Policies governing suspensions might well include not only the provision for suspension but also the firm intent to use the provision when there is no other satisfactory alternative. It should never be used as a threat in personnel administration.

Leaves in the personnel activity. As viewed in this discussion leaves are a part of the personnel activity, in contrast to their professional implications which are covered in another text in the series. In the relationship under consideration here they have two functions, namely, to reduce the staff in size and to serve in a disciplinary action for cause. In either case they may be voluntary or involuntary and will be affected by legal and policy regulations. The tenure and contractual status of staff will have a direct bearing upon whether or not they are eligible for leaves of the type indicated. Such leaves are rarely used but, as in the case of suspension, similar authority to grant leaves should be within the province of the personnel administrator, subject to board review.

Summary. This concludes the discussion of the personnel process or "activity" outlined in Chapters III and IV. This process provides the basic structure of the function of the personnel administrator in the school system. It has been analyzed as an area which should be governed by policy, frequently growing out of legal stipulations, and undergirded by well-developed procedures that have grown through a participatory process involving staff. Most of the process affects staff quite directly and therefore is especially related to morale and staff welfare.

Under such circumstances it is difficult to keep the real objective of all personnel administration—namely, the welfare of children and youth—as a guiding principle. But to do less ignores the reason for the existence of personnel administration.

CHAPTER V

Ethical, Economic, and Contractual Relationships

School personnel are employed and perform their services within the context of legal and other relationships surrounding their immediate activities and of the larger social structure. Their ethical, economic, and contractual relationships are involved. Each of these relationships will be treated separately, although there are many overlappings as they apply to the work of school personnel.

Ethical Relationships

The maturity of a profession is to a very considerable extent measured by the nature of its ethical conduct. Ethical standards evolve out of a long line of experience, the development of leadership in a group, and the realization of the necessity to control the action of the group for its own benefit as well as for its service to society. Experience is a hard teacher and the inevitable conflct between the immediate welfare of a groyp and of the society it serves suggests the principal forces that operate in the development of professional ethics.

Before proceeding further an attempt at defining what is meant by ethics seems in order. Previous reference has been made relating ethics to experience and conduct. Values are a third factor that must be considered. Values are evolved by the society or a group in the society out of its experience as to what is "good" for it. An element of survival is involved. For society to survive it sets up, through custom and law, certain acceptable behavior patterns. Likewise a group, such as teachers, finds out what is "good" for it and evolves a value structure.

Value structures within a sub-group in the society, such as a profession, are affected by the value structures of other groups and of society as a whole. Consequently, there is a constant flux in developing ethical relationships. It is appropriate to look at the stage of the development of ethics in the educational profession, particularly in the public schools, and to note some of the problems of ethics in the current national scene.

Developing ethical standards and practices. While in the final analysis the practice of ethics becomes an individual matter, the problem currently is one closely associated with the organizations with which the teacher and other professional school personnel have associated themselves.

In an effort to improve their services as well as their image, these organizations have made great effort to embody the ethical relationships upon which some agreement can be reached into a "code" that covers the principal areas of contact within the group and the community. In so doing they are using the same techniques as those employed by such groups as lawyers, doctors, clergymen, architects, nurses, public employees, and organized labor.

The problem of agreeing upon a code and policing it is related to the size of the group; it is of one proportion when a group the size of the medical profession is involved and of yet another when the group exceeds one and a half million, as does the educational profession. Another problem that affects the practice of a code is the nature of the employment. Private practice and public employment present very different climates of operation for ethical practice. In the case of public employment there is a likelihood of many ethical relationships being covered by law. In some respects this may reduce the initiative of the group in raising its own ethical standards and policing them.

The ethics of the teaching and associated professional groups can be analyzed under four principal relationships.

The student. This is the primary ethical relationship of the teacher. In behaving ethically with the child the teacher deals justly and considerately with each child and works toward helping him achieve his maximum potential. Unless otherwise required by law, information about students is deemed confidential and the most discreet use is made of it. In dealing with the student the teacher acts professionally, never exploiting his relationship in such areas as tutoring, conferences, and private contacts. The ethical teacher also works with the home and with school and community agencies for the child's benefit.

The community. The ethical teacher recognizes the school as a community institution, and recognizes not only the right and responsibility of the public to participate in the formulation of educational policy but also his own obligation to practice full political and citizenship responsibilities. He feels obligated to protect the educational program from undesirable infringement and exploitation and helps make known the needs of the school in order that it may render a maximum service. He also recognizes that the school system operates under policies established through board and administrative channels, and while privileged to participate in their development, he is obligated to follow these policies.

The profession. It is through the united effort of his profession that the ethical teacher assumes the opportunity and responsibility for improving its ethical conduct and thus its image and over-all influence. He recognizes, as in the practice of his general citizenship, that he must participate in professional activities and be willing to stand their consequences. He recognizes his responsibility for strengthening the profession through selective recruitment, participation in teacher training activities, and helping colleagues, particularly new teachers, in handling professional problems. While not charged with this as an individual, he will assume his share of responsibility for obtaining fair and equitable treatment for himself and others who work with him. He will maintain an ethical relationship with his colleagues in seeking advancement. He also recognizes his responsibility for intellectual and professional honesty in handling teaching and professional issues and problems.

Professional employment practices. This area of professional ethics, closely associated with the third section of this chapter on contractual relationships, deals with applying for a position only if there is a vacancy, adhering to the conditions of a contract unless it is terminated legally or by mutual consent, and conducting professional business through recognized educational and professional channels. Increasingly it may mean associating oneself with a school system only if the working climate is conducive to rendering sound professional service. As teaching becomes a better paid profession, its ethics will no doubt discourage outside employment which impairs professional effectiveness.

It should be noted that the professional group cannot entirely control professional employment practices. Local board policies, administrative practices, community climate, and precedent affect the exercise of good ethical behavior. A commitment to improve such conditions may be regarded as an ethical responsibility for a professional teacher.

Increasingly the issues of sanctions, boycotts, and strikes are involved with the ethics of professional employment practices. There is no place within the ethical position of any recognized professional organization for such practices unless all other possibilities have been exhausted.

Variety of organizations and practices. There is no single organization that can speak for all professional teachers. Consequently, ethical concepts are in some variety. The highly local organization of education in this country, too, makes for a wide interpretation and practice of professional ethics. These numerous facts, coupled with the fact that teachers are public employees, suggest the probability that a tight code of ethics with effective enforcement, is unlikely, or at least very far in the future.

Economic Relationships

The determination of the pay of teachers and other educational personnel in the public schools has been a controversial question throughout the history of our school system. It has been so particularly in recent years when the economic structure has undergone rapid growth and the systems of taxation and support for education have been hard put to keep up with the changes.

The controversial aspects of the problem may be classified largely under two headings: (1) the amount of pay and (2) the nature of the plan or schedule under which the payments are determined.

In an attempt to deal satisfactorily with both problems a brief look at the kind of enterprise with which we are dealing is appropriate. Looking at it in an economic sense, it is impossible to put a monetary value upon the educational product of the schools. The effect of the school versus the home and the community, as well as the fact that the product has been influenced by many different teachers and schools, and even school systems, serves to illustrate the complicated nature of the problem. Consequently, the wealth that teachers create is not in such form that they can gain control of it or put an immediate value upon it.

Another peculiar condition that limits relating the end product of the schools to the economic system is that the public schools operate as a virtual monopoly, with the salaries of staff coming from the taxpayers. This is in contrast to the business enterprise which is essentially privately controlled and which is operated within a framework of competition and for profit that can be measured in dollars and cents.

In the business field such basic economic laws as those of supply and demand largely operate to control prices and wages. Only in a limited sense, as in the case of extreme over- or under-supply of staff, do they affect teachers' pay. In one sense, of course, supply of staff is controlled. It must be drawn from a certificated group which enters the preparation program four to five years before employment, so the supply-demand relationship is never in balance. Thus the field of education cannot be compared to business and industry, nor can the latter's salary and wage policies and practices be copied for use in school systems. As a result, school systems have found it necessary to develop their own salary and wage policies and these will be treated briefly.

A brief history of teachers' salaries. The history of teachers' salaries represents a long struggle to obtain pay consistent with preparation requirements and the cost and standards of living required of the teacher. A history and summary of the economic status of staff may be found in the *Encyclopedia of Educational Research*[1] which traces the struggle over the period of this century. Drawing heavily upon the work of the Research Division of the National Education Association, it describes the progress of teachers' salaries from an average of about $1300 annually in 1926–27 to $4156 in 1955–56. Since that time there has been a steady climb at an average annual rate of about 5.0 per cent to an estimated $6449 in 1964–65.[2] This reference is revised annually and provides a continuing source of information.

Insofar as the Consumer Price Index is an accurate measure of the increases in the cost of living for staff members throughout the United States, the real gain in the purchasing power of average

---

[1] Harold E. Moore and John E. Burke, "Staff Economic Status," *Encyclopedia of Educational Research* (New York: The Macmillan Company, 1960), pp. 1367–1372.

[2] National Education Association, Research Division, *Estimates of School Statistics, 1964–65* (Washington, D.C.: The Association, 1964), pp. 12–13.

salaries amounts to 40.5 per cent in the 10 years since 1954–55. While this seems substantial, teachers' salaries are always in a position of trying to catch up with the economy and comparable salaries in other professions and government generally.

Averages, too, are misleading. The wide range in salaries between states and school systems within states points up the problem. The 1964–65 state averages show a variation from a low of $4220 in one state to a high of $8300 (excluding Alaska) in another.[3] Regarding this range between the lowest and highest state average, some gain has been achieved since 1954–55 when the ratio between the highest and lowest average state salaries was about 2.3. Despite this decrease in percentage relationship, the dollar gap has widened about $1300 over the 10-year period.

Salary changes do not represent the entire change in economic status. Staff welfare practices in areas other than salaries have changed greatly in recent years. These have been summarized in another volume in The Library of Education Series to which previous reference has been made.[4]

Salary scheduling. In recent years research and study have brought steady improvement in the development of salary schedules for educational staff to go with the improvement in amounts of pay.

Several factors have influenced these changes. The demand for better teachers has raised the amount that citizens and boards of education are willing to pay. Enlightened school administration has taken the leadership in the development of sound principles and policies for paying staff. Teacher and other staff organizations, with the benefit of research and leadership from their state and national organizations, have greatly influenced the principles, policies, and schedules under which their members are paid. The growing economic structure in most sections of the nation has made such improvement possible.

Another factor has had an over-riding influence on all concerned. The urgent need of our nation to have better and better prepared citizens to compete with other economic and political systems in the world has prompted our citizens to pay the cost of education, of which the large part is salaries of staff.

Methods of salary scheduling. Salary scheduling is essentially a

---

3 *Ibid.,* p. 14.
4 Kindred and Woodard, *Staff Welfare Practices in the Public Schools.*

local district function in our organization of public education, although it is influenced by state minimum salary laws found in about two-thirds of the states. Under this condition it is essentially a matter of local board policy. Consequently, there is a wide variation in the factors and how they are used that are involved in salary schedules. Because of the space limitation only a general consideration can be given here to this subject upon which volumes have been written. Generally, salary schedules take into consideration such factors as (1) preparation of the staff member, (2) experience, (3) professional improvement, and (4) success or a recognition factor. Many other factors such as sex, position, dependency, extra pay for extra duties, and longevity considerations are used in some schedules.

The factors most used are preparation and experience. Schedules vary in their use, but the so-called "single salary schedule," which determines the pay of each class of professional employee, of which teachers are in the great majority, is in widest practice. In developing such schedules the number of preparation levels, i.e., bachelor's degree to doctor's degree, and the number of experience steps, i.e., 8 to 20 years, represent the essential differences from system to system. The tendency is to increase the breadth of preparation levels recognized in the schedule and to decrease the number of experience steps to 12 to 14 years.

The other factors—professional improvement and recognition, which will be discussed later—have some degree of influence on the better schedules. It is generally agreed that the factor of continuing professional improvement should be built into and rewarded in salary schedules. How this is done should relate to the level of preparation and experience of the group concerned, as well as to goals the board of education and staff have set for themselves.

One of the important aspects in salary scheduling is the establishment of a relationship between beginning and maximum salaries. There is a strong opinion in the profession that the maximum salary at the master's degree preparation level should be at least twice the beginning salary in the schedule. Sometimes this is accomplished by establishing a "ratio" between them. The ratio can operate vertically and horizontally in the schedule, thus crediting both preparation and experience. The chief advantages of the ratio plan are to make clear the relationship between the beginning and maximum salaries in the schedule and to weight both preparation and experience for the professional teacher. Recent trends in salary scheduling are described in two recent National Education Association Research Bulletins.[5]

One of the most controversial aspects of salary scheduling is dealing with the recognition of superior performance in the classroom and in other aspects of professional service. The term "merit rating" is often attached to this concept. The desirability of recognizing superior teaching performance goes without saying; the manner in which it can be done equitably and at the same time maintain the morale and acceptance of such a plan by the employee group is quite another problem.

Many assume this is a new approach in salary scheduling. Actually school districts have experimented with various approaches to the problem over the last half century. Many more of these systems have dropped the rewarding of a few members of the staff through "merit" determination than have retained the plan. The programs of six school districts with such plans have been researched in a recent study by Steffensen. He observes:

> The effort by many districts with merit salary programs, and this may well apply to those without, to strive for a high degree of specificity in their evaluation procedures is apparent when these procedures are examined. Perhaps this effort is associated with the rather large testing programs carried on in the schools, or with the developments in more efficient teaching devices. And, certainly, salary advances in industry have been closely related to increased productivity per employee. To assume that teacher performance can be measured may be the reflection of a need for greater efficiency in the educational system. To implement this assumption, there must be developed descriptions of the goals of education as well as the responsibilities of the teacher in fulfilling those goals. Whether this can, or more important should, result in the development of measurable criteria of teacher effectiveness as has been suggested, is a question worthy of study.
>
> The entire reward system for teachers is a complex of such factors as salaries, fringe benefits, status, class load, responsibility, and security, among others. The salary structure is obviously an important segment of this total structure. The need for a general elevation

[5] National Education Association, Research Division. *Salary Schedules for Classroom Teachers,* 1964–65, Research Report 1964–E13 (Washington, D.C.: The Association, March 1965).

National Education Association, Research Division, *Index Salary Schedules for Classroom Teachers,* 1964–65, Research Memo 1965–6 (Washington, D.C.: The Association, March 1965).

of salaries as a means of improving instruction through the recruitment and retention of capable teachers is well known. The directions which these improvements should take are of local, State, and national concern.

Of important concern within the total teacher compensation problem is the provision of adequate maximum salaries for teachers which will serve as one incentive to the extent that the schools can compete more satisfactorily than now for their staff. One solution would be to elevate the maximum for the entire profession, assuming that the Nation would be able to support such an effort. If this elevation is to be of a significant amount, it is apparent that necessary funds would be of a prohibitive amount, even if it were a desirable goal.

One alternative to this general raising of the maximums is to provide for some differentiation on a selective basis, presumably according to the performance level. It is at this point in the much larger problem of teacher compensation that the issue of merit salaries enters the discussion. The fact that the encouragement and rewarding of superior performance on a differential salary basis may be accomplished through means other than merit salary policies has been previously stated. Which is the best means is another question. The school districts cooperating with the preparation of this bulletin have accepted the merit salary approach as the most appropriate salary policy. Other districts have approached the problem of salary differentiation through other means.

The merit salary question is but one part of the entire reward system and of the total salary structure. However, it is of sufficient interest as an innovation to warrant its inclusion as one part of any discussion of the total teacher compensation problem.[6]

One of the problems in having any "merit" plan succeed is the opposition of teacher organizations. Their opposition is largely related to the lack of an adequate procedure by which the effectiveness of teaching can be rated for salary purposes. While there has been extensive research in this area by Barr, Ryans, and others, it is generally agreed that no adequate and acceptable procedure for general use has been developed. More experimental programs, carried on in cooperation with staff, are needed. Further discussion of this question may be found in Chapter VI.

Other economic benefits. Previous reference has been made to the fact that salary is not the only economic benefit which rewards

---

[6] James P. Steffensen, *Merit Salary Programs,* Office of Education, Bulletin 1963, No. 5, pp. 46–48 (Washington, D.C.: Superintendent of Documents, U.S. Government Printing Office).

teaching. In the past few years, a wide range of fringe benefits, somewhat similar to those provided for employees in business, industry, and government, have been provided for teachers and other school district employees. In view of the income tax problems, these are especially valuable and more and more employees look upon salary and fringe benefits as a "package" constituting their economic rewards, and relate them to each other.

No detailed treatment of this area of economic benefits will be included here, although it is logically a part of the total problem. This area has already been treated by Kindred and Woodard in their Library of Education volume, *Staff Welfare Practices in the Public Schools.* The reader is referred to this book for a fuller treatment of the so-called "fringe benefits."

Economic and welfare considerations applied to the nonteaching personnel. The trend in school personnel administration is to provide similar welfare consideration to all classes of employees, but to make the salary modifications that are necessary to obtain appropriate services. Such considerations as sick leave, health and accident insurance, retirement, processes of dismissal, and grievance action are treated under common policy insofar as it is possible. Salary considerations must be kept on a different basis because of the wide variation in preparation levels and the responsibilities associated with different positions. So it is common in well-administered school systems to find, for example, all employees under the same retirement system, but with a number of salary schedules depending upon the classification of employees.

Welfare or fringe benefits are especially important in the area of the nonteaching employees. Frequently these benefits make employment by a school system desirable in contrast to industrial or business employment and enables the school system to compete for services of personnel which would not otherwise be available because of the higher wages paid in private employment.

In the administration of salary programs for nonteaching personnel the tendency is to keep such salaries somewhat below the rates paid in business and industry and to offset the difference by providing steady employment, security, and fringe benefits. As an example, many school systems have kept the hourly rate paid to its craft employees in the maintenance program at about 80 per cent of the regular hourly rate in private unionized employment. This relationship, while geared to the local community practice and perhaps, by the process, to living costs, seems to operate in a manner that will permit the school district to recruit and hold satisfactory employees.

Frequently, too, the wages and salaries of nonteaching employees are similar to those in other government agencies, such as city and state governments. In making such comparisons it is necessary for personnel administrators to compare standards for employment, job output, and the welfare and fringe benefit program.

Usually salary schedules of nonteaching employees have a lesser range between the beginning and maximum salary, but the maximum is reached sooner. This is more in keeping with practice in business and industry for similar employees.

The area of personnel administration involving salary and fringe benefits for nonteaching employees has had much less study than is the case with the professional staff. Recently the American Association of School Business Officials (1011 Church Street, Evanston, Illinois) has instituted a research program to care partially for this void. Locally, school study councils such as the Metropolitan School Study Council of Teachers College, Columbia University in New York have made studies on a regional basis that have also aided in improving practices.

Much remains to be done in improving standards for employment, personnel practices, in-service training and supervision, job classification, and salary and fringe benefit programs for the nonteaching personnel.

Contractual Relationships

The contract serves a very important purpose in the personnel operation. Most staff relationships to the school system are covered by contracts. Such contracts usually have their origin in law and school board policy. The terms of such contracts are usually prescribed by law except that assignment, length, and compensation are within the prerogatives of the local board.

Many states have standard contract forms for different types of positions. Such contracts usually designate the responsibilities and privileges of each party to the contract. In this relationship the source of the teacher's right to his job is contractual, not statutory. There is no mystery surrounding such an agreement. It is one which, done in good faith, creates an obligation on both parties. Most state contract forms involving teachers have been developed with legal assistance both from the teachers' representatives and the boards as employing officials.

Most contracts refer to the existing rules and regulations of the board of education and those that may be adopted as being made a part of the contract. Court decisions have supported this position, so teachers would do well to know what is included in such rules and regulations, since they will be bound by them.

While oral contracts made under certain conditions may be legal and enforceable, contracts should be in writing and many states require that they must be before the district can pay any compensation under the contract. It is assumed that each party comes into a contractual situation with "clean hands." For example, if the position requires a certain type of certification, and the teacher signing the contract does not qualify for the certificate, the contract is terminated when the condition is not fulfilled.

Usually legality of the teacher's employment requires not only his signing a contract but also its approval by the board of education in a legally constituted meeting. This latter action is significant both for the teacher and the board, because the latter cannot legally disburse funds until such action takes place.

A more extensive discussion of the law as it affects school employees may be found in Gauerke's *School Law,*[7] another one of The Library of Education Series.

There are three basic types of teacher's contracts; these may also be applicable to other educational personnel. Brief discussions follow concerning each one.

Contract for the probationary teacher. The first employment of a new teacher, or, for the most part, of an experienced teacher if he goes into a new system, is usually probationary. The contract he receives also reflects this character; it has all the force of other types of contracts except that it is for a limited period, usually one year. Ordinarily probation lasts two or three years in a system before the teacher is eligible for a continuing or tenure contract. The purpose of a contract providing for a period of probation is to determine if a teacher or other employee gives satisfactory service. Such a rela-

---

[7] Gauerke, Chapter IV.

tionship permits, and even forces, a review of his service, thus keeping the welfare of those taught in a primary position.

States differ with respect to contract renewal practices during the probationary period, but usually they require annual reappointment. Some states include probationary teachers under the "continuing contract" relationship.

The continuing contract.   A continuing contract of the spring-notification type is another plan for governing the term of employment. This plan requires that the teacher be notified by a specified date if his services are not desired for the following year; otherwise his contract is renewed automatically for at least another year. The responsibility for notification lies with the board of education. This type of contract is distinguished from protective continuing contracts and permanent tenure arrangements chiefly by the fact that it permits dismissal at the end of the year, with no statement of reason, provided the notification has been made in accordance with the provisions of the state statute and local board regulations, if applicable.

This type of contract may even cover the probationary teacher after his first year, and has numerous advantages, including the security offered teachers and the lesser amount of administrative work involved.

There is an overlapping relationship between this type of contract and the tenure contract covered in the following section, in that the practice concerning notification would apply to both those who have not achieved tenure and those who hold tenure contracts.

It is difficult to be very specific on such matters since they are subject to board rules and regulations and, more especially, state laws. The reader should consult pertinent laws and regulations as they relate to this subject.

The tenure contract.   The third type of contract to which we have referred is the tenure contract, provided by statute in most of the states. Currently over two-thirds of employed public school teachers are protected by tenure laws. A statutory requirement that teachers be employed on annual contracts is a "tenure law" in the dictionary sense, but "teacher tenure law" usually refers to statutory provisions securing a position to the teacher except for stated reasons and until the teacher's services are terminated in an orderly way, by a specified procedure.

A teacher is placed under "tenure" after serving a probationary period of typically three, but with ranges from two to five, years, depending upon the state. After securing tenure, the teacher can be dismissed only for cause as stated in the statute and through a procedure also provided by law. In most respects this is a "continuing contract" and the term is sometimes confused with the tenure relationship. However, some states have "continuing contracts" of the spring-notification type, described in the previous section, and do not have "tenure" in the sense used here.

The objectives of tenure have been announced by the National Education Association Committee on Tenure and Academic Freedom as follows:

1. To protect classroom teachers and other members of the teaching profession against unjust dismissal of any kind—political, religious, or personal

2. To prevent the management or domination of the schools by political or non-educational groups for selfish and other improper purposes

3. To secure for the teacher employment conditions which will encourage him to grow in the full practice of his profession, unharried by constant pressure and fear

4. To encourage competent, independent thinkers to enter and to remain in the teaching profession

5. To encourage school management, which might have to sacrifice the welfare of the schools to fear and favor, to devote itself to the cause of education

6. To set up honest, orderly, and definite procedures by which undesirable people may be removed from the teaching profession

7. To protect educators in their efforts to promote the financial and educational interests of public-school children

8. To protect teachers in the exercise of their rights and duties of American citizenship

9. To enable teachers, in spite of reactionary minorities, to prepare children for life in a republic under changing conditions.[8]

The above reference cites many court decisions with respect to the several types of tenure laws. One of the stronger laws is the Indiana statute that the United States Supreme Court has construed as providing a continuing contractual obligation unless the teacher is dismissed for cause. Other states, such as Illinois, have statutes that provide tenure, but the court decisions have ruled that the con-

---

[8] National Education Association, Research Division, *Trends in Teacher Tenure Legislation and Court Decisions* (Washington, D.C.: The Association, 1959), p. 8.

tractual rights obtained were private rights that would have to yield to the public welfare if the legislature saw fit to change the law.

Usually the tenure relationships relate to a school district, but a few state-wide tenure laws provide that a teacher, having obtained tenure, retains tenure status when he moves to another district in the same state. This is an example of how varied are the tenure laws and how each law is a case in itself.

Dismissal of a tenure teacher can be only for causes as enumerated in the law and typically are incompetence, neglect of duty, unprofessional conduct, immorality, insubordination, and physical disability. Usually, too, the dismissal can take place if there is a justifiable reduction in the size of staff. Often in such cases tenure laws provide an orderly manner for reduction such as:

1. A permanent teacher may not be dismissed while a probationary teacher is retained in a position which the tenure teacher is qualified to fill
2. Permanent teachers must be dismissed in reverse order of employment
3. Permanent teachers so dismissed are to be re-employed before probationary teachers are added to the staff
4. Permanent teachers so dismissed are to be re-employed in order of length of service.[9]

Most tenure laws define specifically the procedure that must be followed in a dismissal action. Each law is different but the steps are typically (1) notification in writing with a statement of cause, (2) provision for a "hearing" within a reasonable time, (3) a provision for notification of dismissal or reinstatement after the hearing, and (4) provision for appeal over the school board's action. Each of these steps must be a formal legal one. Procedural errors are frequently used to invalidate a dismissal action.

With respect to the right to appeal there are several types of appeal bodies. Typically they are (1) to a county or state educational authority, (2) to a state board of education, (3) to tenure commissions established by law, and (4) to the courts. Each state tenure law defines its own appeal procedure. If the appeal reaches the courts the appellant has the typical rights under the law.

The problem in summarizing a complicated area such as the tenure relationship is that it may appear that the summary will

---

9 *Ibid.*, p. 25.

apply generally. The generalizations have been used as illustrative and the student is urged to consult his state law and any pertinent court decisions concerning it to obtain its specific applications.

Summary. The emphasis in this section has been to demonstrate the place and importance of contracts in the staffing of the public schools. Each staff member is subject to one or more contractual relationships and should be familiar with the legal privileges and requirements under which he works.

CHAPTER VI

Morale, Recognition, and Appraisal Considerations in Personnel Administration

The grouping of three significant relationships in this chapter is not an accidental one; they are being considered with relation to each other because of their character and nature. All are deeply involved with human values, deal with highly intangible factors, and are especially subject to emotional reaction. They are strongly associated with job satisfaction and dissatisfaction and are related to the rewards, both monetary and personal, for educational service.

Another common characteristic of the three considerations is the problem of quantifying them. While an increasing amount of research and study has gone on, especially in the past ten years, it is recognized that much remains to be done before adequate measures and procedures are available to serve and guide the personnel administrator as he works with these fields.

Each consideration will be treated in a separate section in this chapter, with appropriate references to the others. Because of their intangible nature, many of the relationships will require careful thought on the part of the reader.

The Morale of Staff

Increasingly, one of the principal roles of administration, and particularly personnel administration, is seen as releasing the creative capacities of staff. To a very considerable extent staff performance over and above the minimal depends upon the intangible factor called "morale." One of the difficulties in dealing with this subject is the wide range of meaning that individuals and groups place upon it. Despite this problem there have been increasing interest and study in the field during the last decade.

Recognizing the importance of morale, educators adapted the

results of studies in industry, the armed services, and other groups to staff morale problems in the field of education.

The large number of studies in recent years in the field of education has moved in the direction of (1) attempts to define morale, (2) attempts to measure morale, (3) attempts to relate the level of morale with the quality of education, (4) attempts to relate morale to school and community structure, and (5) studies of staff attitudes as they relate to the numerous factors affecting the personal and professional life of staff.

Attempts to define morale. A dictionary definition of the term "morale" suggests the elements that are in or related to it. The definition says it refers to "condition as affected by or dependent upon such moral or mental factors as zeal, spirit, hope, pride, confidence, etc." The difficulty of applying such intangible factors as these in morale studies has resulted in the development of operational approaches, in which the feelings, opinions, and attitudes of staff are explored. Morale is also expressed in behavior, which is at least to a limited degree observable and measurable.

Consequently, feelings, opinions, attitudes, and behavior usually form the basis for an operational definition of morale. How these are put together to form a definition depends largely upon the authority and the situation.

Any attempt to define morale should be related to whether individual or group morale is under consideration. Some persons seem less affected by the group relationship than others, and continue to function at a high level in spite of conditions which lower the morale of the group.

It would appear in such cases that individual values supersede those of the group. The point is made to establish the importance of values and goals in studying morale in the individual or group, and to relate them to an operational definition of morale.

From these statements an operational definition of morale, applied to a given situation, must be developed. Broadly speaking the definition will be concerned with the satisfactions and dissatisfactions associated with the situation.

Implications for personnel administration. The study of morale is so interesting and challenging that there is a temptation to report all the numerous recent studies and writings in morale as applied to the educational staff. It is believed the more useful approach is to attempt to note the implications of some of the studies and their application to school personnel administration.

Areas involving morale studies. Since individuals and groups vary widely in their reaction to individual factors affecting morale, patterns of conditions affecting morale are discernible in various situations. This approach was used by Redefer and others in a group of studies at New York University.[1] Three major areas for intensive studies through fifty individual projects were set up. Twenty-four school systems, involving approximately 5000 teachers, voluntarily took part in the series of studies. Using five carefully prepared questionnaires and opinionnaires a "Morale Tendency Score" was developed for each teacher. The term "tendency" was used because of the limitations in obtaining an absolute numerical score that would measure morale. The upper and lower quarters of the resulting distribution of the teacher population of each school system as well as of the total group were given special consideration. The upper quarter resulting from positively toned responses was called the "high morale teachers" and the lower quarter was called "low morale teachers."

The areas covered by the instruments were entitled (1) About You and Your School, (2) You and Your Faculty, (3) About You as a Professional Person, (4) Social and Professional Relations, (5) If You Were, and (6) Speaking Frankly.

The six instruments explored approximately 350 relationships of each teacher to his school, the faculty, his social and professional associates and organization, and the faculty structure.

While an important beginning, the lack of an established reliability for the instruments, as well as uncertainty with respect to their validity, suggests caution in their use.

Factors that affect morale. The series of studies by Redefer and others refer to the numerous factors that affect morale. Van Zwoll has summarized the findings of 25 authors who have written about or researched the morale of the educational staff. He has organized his findings concerning morale factors as follows: organization, administration, environment, worker correlates, operation, objectives, work load, and others.[2]

---

[1] National Education Association, Research Division, *The Morale of Teachers* (prepared by Dr. Frederick L. Redefer), Research Memo, 1963–18 (Washington, D.C.: The Association, 1963), p. 48.

[2] Van Zwoll, *School Personnel Administration,* p. 170.

Generally the concern of researchers in morale studies has been to identify the variables or clusters of variables that will reveal the morale status of staff. Since morale varies with groups and situations, the researcher is faced with working with more than one unknown— a kind of human quadratic equation.

There is danger that concern for the morale of one group, such as teachers, may overshadow that for other staff components. For example, certain research studies have revealed that the principal in an elementary school is a key to staff morale. For the personnel administrator to overlook the principal in an effort to build morale in the staff would be to lose the most valuable ally in morale development.

These statements reveal the complications in morale consideration. They also suggest the necessity on the part of the personnel administrator to seek and use the active participation and cooperation of the several components of the staff. The importance of considering research findings as well as using action research appropriate to the local situation cannot be overemphasized.

Morale and the working environment. The goal of personnel administration is a staff with high morale—one which accomplishes the purposes of education. The nature of staff morale is one of the best means of judging a level of achievement. There have been many efforts to describe the type of working environment that would obtain such results. There has been no better summary than the following:

1. A feeling on the part of each person that his contribution is accorded merit by the group
2. A feeling that the organization to which he belongs is making a worthy contribution to the welfare of society
3. A feeling that he is becoming increasingly competent
4. A feeling that all members of the group are being fairly treated
5. Assurance that the channels of communication are free and open and will be used in reaching decisions
6. A feeling on the part of each person that he is participating in all aspects of a job.[3]

Such elements as staff participation in policy making and planning, communication, good human relations, a goal-centered organization,

---

[3] Metropolitan School Study Council, *The School Staff,* rev. ed., by Committee of Staff Members from the Council Schools (New York, 1952), p. 20.

well-defined duties and responsibilities, good physical working conditions, personal, economic, and academic security, a feeling of growth and achievement, and good interpersonal relations appear over and over in such lists and in the studies previously noted in this chapter. It would appear that (1) there is clear evidence that morale is important; (2) the factors and elements affecting morale can be identified; (3) morale can be measured well enough to deal with problems related to it—though not absolutely; (4) administration, the board, and community are key agents in improving morale; and (5) there is a relationship between morale and good educational achievement by students.

These conclusions warrant an important place for dealing with morale in the hierarchy of duties assigned to the personnel administrator, although it is recognized that he alone cannot deal with its many facets and relationships.

Appraisal and Recognition of the Effectiveness of Teaching

Closely related to the morale of the teaching staff is the problem of appraising and recognizing the effectiveness of teaching. Probably no aspect of education has been discussed with greater frequency, with more emotion, and from a base of less objectivity. This reaction grows out of the fact that there is no common agreement on standards to be used as the criteria of teacher effectiveness. The problem is also aggravated by the frequent attempts to associate pay schedules with effectiveness or "merit," a term frequently used in salary schedules, and to which reference is made in Chapter V. If the salary aspect could be separated from determining teacher effectiveness there would be a greater chance that it could be determined.

Research in teacher performance appraisal. The research on this subject is usually discussed under two headings: (1) criteria of teacher effectiveness, and (2) the prediction of teacher effectiveness.

Our concern in this volume is primarily with the first, although this is in no sense to discount the importance of the second.

After surveying the literature on the criteria of teacher effectiveness Mitzel observes, "More than a half-century of research effort has not yielded meaningful, measurable criteria around which the majority of the nation's educators can rally."[4] The article goes on to state that "teacher effectiveness as a concept has no meaning apart from the criterion measures or operational definitions of success as a teacher. These measures should possess four basic attributes: (a) relevance, (b) reliability, (c) freedom from bias, and (d) practicality."

In an effort to clarify such basic attributes, a Committee on the Criteria of Teacher Effectiveness, organized by the American Educational Research Association in 1950, published two reports which have done a great deal to develop the concepts and provide a terminology that has sharpened the recent research in this area.[5]

In summarizing the classification of criteria, Mitzel lists three general areas: (1) product criteria, (2) process criteria, and (3) presage criteria.[6] The first refers to judging effectiveness by the extent of "student change" as related to the goals of the schools, such as growth in learning. The second is behavioral in nature and relates to judging the worthwhile changes in student and teacher behavior, such as teacher-pupil rapport or disciplinary relationships. The third is even less tangible and refers to such variables as (1) teacher personality, (2) teacher training characteristics, (3) teacher knowledge and achievement, and (4) in-service teacher status characteristics.

The nature of the criteria described above, which have evolved after much laborious research, suggests the complicated nature of the problem. It is evident from these criteria that the problem is a multi-dimensional one, and should involve wide staff participation in the appraisal process.

Research is continuing which throws some light on the problem. The extensive research by Ryans on teacher characteristics[7] and by Barr on measurement and prediction are good examples of such continuing effort.[8]

Applying the research.   Despite the inconclusive nature of the

[4] Harold E. Mitzel, "Teacher Effectiveness," *Encyclopedia of Educational Research* (New York: The Macmillan Company, 1960), p. 1481.

[5] H. H. Remmers, (Ch.), "Report of the Committee on the Criteria of Teacher Effectiveness," *Review of Educational Research* XXII, pp. 238–63 and LXIII, pp. 641–658, 1953.

[6] Mitzel, *Encyclopedia of Educational Research,* pp. 1482–1485.

[7] David B. Ryans, "Investigation of Teacher Characteristics," *Educational Record,* XXXIV, 1953, pp. 370–96.

[8] A. S. Barr, *Wisconsin Studies of Measurement and Prediction of Teacher Effectiveness* (Madison: Dunbar Publications, Inc., 1961).

research studies, school personnel administrators are compelled to make decisions and work out operational relationships, and in some cases even develop "merit pay" plans.

The difficulties involved should be taken as a challenge and techniques should be developed whereby the teaching staff, administrative personnel, and boards of education work together to formulate goals, provide fullest participation, and evaluate the results of any plans that are cooperatively developed.

If such efforts can be seen as "professional development" instead of merit pay programs, more progress seems possible. More leadership should come out of the profession itself on this issue. Growth and development are personal and individual concerns, and administration- or board of education-imposed programs of evaluation are often defeated even before they are initiated. The important element in the appraisal program is the objective. Cooperatively defined criteria of good teaching rather than techniques or devices must be uppermost in the minds of those concerned. Fear of appraisal must be dispelled; any plan used can be successful only if there is the widest possible acceptance of it in the staff. Self-appraisal should be a built-in aspect of any program. Researchers and administrators alike must recognize that the theoretical findings of research are often useless in a climate of unsatisfactory personnel policies and working conditions. They will also need to recognize that there is no one absolute and easy answer to determining teacher effectiveness since teaching requires a technical knowledge of applied pedagogical science and the creative, highly individualized approach of an artist. Despite this, teaching does not require persons of superhuman ability, so the effort to work out operational plans for appraising teacher effectiveness need not be a search for an unrealizable paragon.

Other methods of recognition. Fortunately not all recognition of the success of a teacher comes through a critical evaluation of his classroom teaching effectiveness. There are some very tangible factors that can and should be recognized. His devotion to duty, his community relations, his service in the many extra duties which relate to the teacher's job, his continued growth through in-service training are a few. These are reasonably evident, provided some agreed-upon goals are set up against which they may be judged.

Community acceptance and status are also means of recognizing the worth of teachers. School boards, under administrative leadership, frequently provide programs for recognizing exceptional service. The difficulty of most community and board plans is the limited extent of their application and the means by which persons are selected. Peer nominations, based on group-developed goals, offer a built-in encouragement for unselfish service on the part of staff.

Summary. The inadequate communication and cooperative effort in developing plans for appraisal and recognition continues to be the most serious problem, not only as it relates to the effectiveness of such plans but also to the morale of staff that is involved. A recent National Education Association Research Bulletin[9] has indicated that one of the surprising results of their study was the extent to which teachers were unfamiliar with the means by which they were evaluated and the very general nature of most evaluations. The extent of the use of such terms as "satisfactory," "unsatisfactory," "poor," "fair," or "excellent," without adequate definition of the meaning of the terms as used by the evaluator was revealed. There is not much promise for continuing growth on the part of staff under such conditions.

It should not be indicated that there is no good work going on in this area. Many school systems have groups giving regular attention to the problem. The publication of *Who's a Good Teacher,*[10] by the American Association of School Administrators, is also representative of the continuing efforts of professional organizations to clarify the issues and provide communication to teachers, school boards, and the public.

---

[9] National Education Association, Research Division, *Evaluation of Classroom Teachers* Research Report R–14, 1964 (Washington, D.C.: The Association, 1964).
[10] American Association of School Administrators, *Who's a Good Teacher?* (Washington, D.C.: The Association, 1961).

CHAPTER VII

Staff and School Board Relationships

All aspects of personnel administration pertain in the broad sense to staff relationships. This chapter involves those aspects of staff and school board relationships that are concerned with the interaction of school boards, administrators, and classroom teachers in which an equilibrium is being sought within the total power structure represented by the groups. This represents a relatively new dimension in personnel relationships in education and in many respects constitutes the greatest challenge for personnel administration.

Conditions Affecting Staff Relations

At different stages in our history the school boards and/or the school administrators have dominated the power structure of schools. Currently the teaching staff is, through organized activity, becoming a stronger and stronger force, thus causing a re-alignment of relationships within the power structure referred to above.

This is not an overnight change. Depending upon the local situation there always have been various degrees of strength on the part of teacher groups, but at no time in our history has the situation approached the confrontations that now are taking place. These confrontations have led to the extremes involving sanctions, strikes, boycotts, and several instances where teachers have limited their services strictly to classroom activities.

It is not alone a teacher-administrator or a teacher-board confrontation that is taking place. The clashes have included board-administrator differences leading to dismissals, resignations, and suspensions of administrators, and investigation by ethics committees of these relationships.

Deeply involved in all such activities, be they concerned with administrators or teachers, is a strong movement in many communities to wrest control of education from professionals in education.

This situation suggests that the foregoing problems have their grounding in the society, and this is very true.

Political and social systems on a world and national basis have been in conflict. Within the industrial and business world, labor and management have struggled to obtain a greater share of the profits. Even in government, employee groups have, through organization, become an increasing force in affecting their salaries and working conditions. It is not unexpected that the million and a half teachers should increasingly make themselves felt.

This problem is not entirely involved with groups to which we have referred. There is a struggle within the teacher group for power. The National Education Association and its affiliates and the American Federation of teachers (AFL-CIO) are, in many situations—the big cities especially—locked in a struggle to determine which group will represent teachers in their negotiations with administrators and school boards. Divisions of the type noted cause many difficulties for local boards and school administrators, who usually have a policy of freedom for teachers to belong to either organization. If both organizations seek the right to represent the entire body of teachers with the board, this policy is difficult to maintain.

Another situation that affects the interaction of staff with boards and administrators is the general atmosphere in the society that encourages freedom to express oneself and to belong to and participate in organizations so long as they do not advocate the overthrow of the government. A century ago it would have been impossible for a teacher group to face a school board, much less a governor and a legislature, and demand an improvement in educational conditions in the state, but the recent situations involving sanctions in Utah and Oklahoma are illustrative of such actions today.

Teacher groups also have initiated investigations of local conditions that impede educational progress and consideration of their requests. The National Commission on Professional Rights and Responsibilities of the National Education Association has conducted investigations in dozens of school districts, bringing to light conditions that require attention and correction.

The several circumstances that have been described briefly constitute the climate in which staff relationships operate and in which they will be considered in this chapter. Every local situation will be different since the degree of activity, as well as the strength and leadership of the groups involved, will provide its own climate.

Collective action and staff relationships. Collective action in reaching individual and group goals is characteristic of our society. The use of this tool in staff relationships in education is relatively new and school boards, administrators, and teaching staffs are in the process of learning how to use and live with it. Looking back over the past half century there is ample evidence of similar experiences in business and industry. Our industrial history is replete with head-on clashes between management and labor. The sophistication that both of these groups have obtained in settling their problems suggests the possibilities that are ahead for settling staff problems in education. In the meantime there will be breakdowns in local and state relationships that will adversely affect the education of children. The inevitable goal should be to find ways to use collective action without harming the institution that it must serve.

The analogy that has been drawn between the problems of staff relations in education and those in business and industry is not entirely applicable. The teacher is a public employee. State laws usually govern public employees and limit their rights to organize, negotiate, and take punitive action if their demands are ignored. This being the case, teacher groups find themselves in a precarious legal position if they take strong stands. This is leading to new legal patterns so far as teacher groups are concerned. Certain states recently have proposed bills to their legislatures to clarify these relationships. One state, Wisconsin, has gone so far as to place teachers and other school employees under its labor relations legislation.

A recent review of collective action by public school teachers by Wildman describes the relationships and problems in this developing area.[1] Wildman has also written perceptively concerning the implications of collective action on school administration.[2]

Several practices related to this type of action will be given brief consideration. Their discussion is in no way an advocacy of their use since every local situation is subject to specific consideration.

Professional negotiations with school boards. This tool in the

---

[1] Wesley A. Wildman, "Collective Action by Public School Teachers," *Industrial and Labor Relations Review*, XVIII, No. 1 (October 1964).

[2] Wesley A. Wildman, "Implications of Teacher Bargaining for Administrators," *Phi Delta Kappan*, XLVI, No. 4 (December 1964), 152.

collective action category is strongly advocated and frequently used by National Education Association affiliates. In effect it provides a written plan whereby the professional association, through democratically selected representatives using professional channels, participate with administrators and boards of education in the formulation of policies of common concern, including salary and other conditions of service. As noted, such a relationship recognizes the legal responsibility of the board of education, the administrative function of the superintendent, and the professional competencies of teachers in viewing matters of mutual concern.

Many different kinds of agreements have evolved within the framework of negotiations. They range in degree and coverage from agreements on single items, usually salary, to broader coverage involving salary, working conditions, and educational policy, e.g., class size. Usually such agreements define staff and administrative interests and provide joint working relations on designated issues. While modified, the administrative function is not ignored in such agreements. Each agreement is affected by local school board policy and state law as well as by the aggressiveness and leadership in teacher organizations. A recent report by the Research Division of the National Education Association deals with the legal aspects of this issue.[3] The National Education Association has also issued a booklet called *Guidelines for Professional Negotiations.*[4]

At this time at least four states have passed laws legalizing "negotiations." In Connecticut recently enacted legislation requires school boards to hold a representative election upon petition of twenty per cent or more of the certificated staff to determine the organization with which they will negotiate. The new law also provides for a mediation procedure through the office of the state commissioner of education. No doubt some of these new laws will be subject to court tests which will further clarify the authority of the board of education and the other relationships which are involved.

Sanctions.   Another collective action tool advocated in extreme cases by the National Education Association for its affiliates is the

---

[3] National Education Association, Research Division, *Professional Negotiations with School Boards: A Legal Analysis and Review* (Washington, D.C.: The Association, January 1962).

[4] National Education Association, Office of Professional Development and Welfare, *Guidelines for Professional Negotiations,* rev. ed. (Washington, D.C.: The Association, 1965), p. 9.

sanction. The meaning of the term as used by this professional organization follows:

> Sanctions means censure, suspension or expulsion of a member; severance of relationship with an affiliated association or other agency; imposing of a deterrent against a board of education or other agency controlling the welfare of the schools; bringing into play forces that will enable the community to help the board or agency to realize its responsibility; or the application of one or more steps in the withholding of services.

The same reference further states:

> Sanctions are used only to improve educational opportunities through the elimination of conditions detrimental to effective education. The most severe types of sanctions should be invoked only as a last resort where conditions are such that it is impossible for educators to give effective professional service.[5]

The most discussed "sanction" is the one in Utah. Initiated by the Utah Education Association after lengthy efforts to secure certain school improvements, and supported by the National Education Association, the matter became a public and political issue resulting in major improvements, through legislative action, in support of education in Utah. The story has been widely publicized and described in such publications as *Utah: A State-wide Study of School Conditions,*[6] and *Utah School Crisis 1963.*[7] Recently sanctions were invoked in Oklahoma by the Oklahoma Education Association and the National Education Association.

Collective bargaining. This procedure is advocated by The American Federation of Teachers (AFL-CIO) "as a means for winning goals and not the goal itself."[8] Collective bargaining, while a familiar term due to its use in industry, is relatively new in its application to public education. In defining it, its advocates say that collective bargaining may be termed the negotiations between employer and employee representatives on the basis of equality of both groups. It recognizes an economic democracy where both sides of the table

---

[5] *Ibid.*

[6] National Education Association, National Commission on Professional Rights and Responsibilities, *Utah: A State-wide Study of School Conditions* (Washington, D.C.: The Association, March 1963).

[7] John C. Evans, Jr., *Utah School Crisis 1963* (Salt Lake City: Utah Education Association, 1963).

[8] Carl J. Megel, *Collective Bargaining Contracts* (Chicago: The American Federation of Teachers, 1963), Foreword.

have a right in the final decision affecting salaries, working conditions, et cetera.

George M. Harrison defined this type of negotiation in an article entitled "Procedures in Collective Bargaining." Collective bargaining being a group instrument, individuals must come together in groups to assert their democratic right to a voice in establishing the rules which will govern their own employer-employee relationship. This is all that is meant by the term collective bargaining."[9]

The National Labor Relations Act outlines four basic principles of collective bargaining in private employment. They are:

1. A bargaining agent is selected (usually by secret ballot) by a majority of the employees in a bargaining unit. (Bargaining unit refers to the group of employees, clerks, carpenters, musicians, et cetera for whom the agent is to negotiate.)

2. The employers must arrange for a conference when requested by the bargaining agent and they must bargain exclusively with the agent chosen by the majority in the unit

3. The employer must negotiate on all particulars in the controversy submitted but he is not required to agree on any of them

4. The terms agreed upon are written into a contract for an exact period of time.

In elaborating on his position as it relates to the comparison of private employment to that of the public school employment Porter states:

> Collective bargaining in the public schools may not be exactly in the same form as that described by the National Labor Relations Act in private industry. It is foolish to pretend, however, that teachers do not have grievances or problems which need to be negotiated. Bargaining with as many of the rights granted to workers in private industry as possible should be extended to teachers.[10]

One of the characteristics of collective bargaining between teacher groups and boards of education is the anomalous position in which it places school administration. Teacher unions generally insist that their bargaining be directly with the school board, thus ignoring or at least depreciating the administrative function. This creates a special problem for personnel administration in that it is reduced to a negotiating rather than a managing relationship.

---

[9] Quoted in Robert G. Porter, *Collective Bargaining for Teachers, The American Federation of Teachers,* October, 1957, p. 2.

[10] *Ibid.,* p. 2.

The character of collective bargaining contracts is of interest. Such contracts are usually in great detail and they may deal with a wide range of subjects, but grievance procedures, salary schedules, and working conditions are always emphasized. The reader is referred to *Collective Bargaining Contracts,*[11] which describes five contracts, including the one in New York City, in great detail.

Another consideration with respect to collective bargaining in the public schools is its legal status. States differ widely in their laws governing the authority of school boards on this subject and the court decisions have not fully established the perimeters of such action.

The limited strike.   To a degree this procedure relates both to sanctions and strikes and can result only where there is strong collective action, it is a power technique that some organizations have used effectively. Both NEA- and AFT-related groups have been involved in or threatened the limited strike. In this process teachers perform only minimum services, e.g., classroom teaching, and do not perform extra duties such as sponsoring extra-curricular activities. If at all acceptable, it has the advantage of not providing a school stoppage and yet the public is made aware of an impending crisis. It may open the way to negotiations and preserve a major public interest. While the use of "raw power" leaves much to be desired, such limited action may prevent even greater extremes in its use.

The strike issue.   Present in any collective action consideration is the use of the ultimate punitive action by the group in the form of a "strike." The term is so commonplace as it is used in industry that a definition is unnecessary. While the right to strike is available as an action by the personnel in private employment, that right is expressly denied to public employees on the grounds of the vital importance of the public services and the sovereignty of the state and its political sub-divisions. Both the NEA and the AFT have adopted policy statements renouncing the use of the strike. The AFT in its resolution #79 adopted in its Annual Convention in 1963 recognized the right of its locals to strike under certain circumstances. Despite these positions, some teacher strikes have occurred and many more have been threatened.

Drawing upon Bureau of Labor statistics, the author reported, in

---

[11] Megel, *Collective Bargaining Contracts,* p. 14.

a recent address to the Arizona School Boards Association, that there had been 91 strikes by public school teachers from 1940 to 1962. These strikes resulted, according to the Bureau, in the loss of 251,600 man days during the 22-year period.[12]

When strikes develop, both parties are usually responsible. It should be recognized that school boards have strong legal sanctions of their own which they can utilize to protect their interests.

School boards have acted through their national organization in a resolution which follows:

> The authority of the board of education is established by law and this authority may not be delegated to others. Strikes, sanctions, boycotts, mandated arbitration or mediation are improper procedures to be used by public school employees who are dissatisfied with their conditions of employment.
>
> School boards, subject to the requirements of applicable law, shall refrain from compromise agreements based on negotiation or collective bargaining, and shall not resort to mediation or arbitration, nor yield to threats of reprisal on all matters affecting local public schools, including the welfare of all personnel. They shall also resist by all lawful means the enactment of laws which would compel them to surrender any part of their responsibility.[13]

This position supported by a legal structure constitutes a challenge to the increased aggressiveness of the organized personnel.

Organized school personnel do not possess such formal sanctions and, if they stay in legal bounds, must confine themselves to cooperative action short of the strike. This imbalance suggests that while strikes seem incompatible with the field of public education, there is need for legal means by which disputes can be resolved. The public interest is apparent, and while the local board of education is supposed to represent this interest, situations may develop where it is defending its position in contrast to acting in the public interest.

This whole area is one in which great sanity on the part of both parties is necessary if extremes inconsistent with the interest of both parties in the education of children are to be avoided.

The school personnel must also view its own motives and consider whether the teacher strike is an acceptable action. The several rami-

---

[12] Harold E. Moore, "New Wine in Old Bottles," *The Arizona Administrator*, III, No. 4, April 1965, 5.

[13] National School Boards Association, *Policy Statements*, Adopted April 1963, Denver, Colorado.

fications of this problem are discussed by Lieberman in a recent issue of the *Phi Delta Kappan*.[14]

In the New York City Board of Education–American Federation of Teachers agreement, the following no-strike pledge, covering only the contract period, may be found:

> The Union and the Board recognize that strikes and other forms of work stoppages by the teachers are contrary to law and public policy. The Union and the Board subscribe to the principle that differences shall be resolved by peaceful and appropriate means without interruption to the school program. The Union therefore agrees that there shall be no work stoppages or other concerted refusal to perform work by the employees covered by this agreement, nor any instigation thereof.[15]

Collective action and the public image. Since the support of education depends to such a great extent on its public image, the effect of collective action by public school personnel becomes an important consideration. The relationship of the public and the organizations involved in collective action is reflected in the following quotation from Gibson and Hunt:

> School personnel may also have recourse to public opinion at various points in the political process and in the formulation of legislation. Mention has already been made of some of the problems involved in political activity by public employees. Insofar as the political process is intended to provide a forum for accommodating various public interests, it supplies devices such as the lobby and dissemination of persuasive material via public communications media which can serve to shape public opinion and legislative acts. If, however, school personnel confine their activities to matters of their own welfare, they may create a public image which highlights self-centered interests and so detract from their professional role.[16]

In a speech to the American Federation of Teachers (AFL-CIO) Calvin Gross, then superintendent of schools in New York City, said:

> Up until now teachers have always been too complaisant, too docile, too willing to let themselves be put upon. I personally welcome the new show of vigor and muscle which has now become

---

[14] Myron Lieberman, "Teacher Strikes: Acceptable Strategy?" *Phi Delta Kappan*, XLVI, No. 5, January 1965, 237 ff.

[15] Megel, *Collective Bargaining Contracts*, p. 14.

[16] R. Oliver Gibson and Herold C. Hunt, *The School Personnel Administrator* (Boston: Houghton Mifflin Company, 1965), p. 393.

apparent in many parts of our profession. But I would also counsel the use of wisdom and foresight—and the careful exercise of responsibility—as we work out together new ways of rebuilding school systems which have lost their former excellence.[17]

It is difficult to generalize on the effect of collective action by teachers since what may be acceptable in one community might be totally unacceptable in another. In a highly labor-organized industrial community a collective action might be regarded as a way of life. In suburbia it might be regarded as a wholly unacceptable approach to settling differences. Certainly the comments from the editorials of several New York papers in September 1963 concerning the city's experience suggest how the public reacts. Representative of these comments is the one from the New York *Post* of September 9, 1963:

> Before we all relax it would be prudent to take a look at a bargaining procedure which brought us to the brink of chaos. The process is not very satisfactory. Collective bargaining between teachers who are forbidden by law to strike and a board which does not have the final say over how much money it will have to distribute is a contradiction in terms.
>
> That the city came through this time without disaster is no guarantee it will be this fortunate two years from now.
>
> We can all heave a sigh of relief. But we would be guilty of extreme shortsightedness if we did not immediately put our best minds to work devising a better way to settle these matters in the future.

Apparently no one is ever very proud of having an impasse lead to an overt act that stops the educational process. It is hard to see how anyone's image is anything but tarnished after such an experience.

In its publication on *Roles, Responsibilities, Relationships of the School Board, Superintendent, and Staff,* the American Association of School Administrators states:

> We believe that both the board and the professional staff—teachers, principals, and other administrators—should, at a time that is free from tension and controversy, develop together a plan to be used in case of persistent disagreement. In those few, highly unusual instances where major controversy threatens to disrupt the schools, an appeal to an unbiased body should be available to either the board or the teachers, or both. The function of this third party

---

[17] Calvin E. Gross, in address to the 47th Annual Convention of the American Federation of Teachers (AFL-CIO), New York, August, 1963.

should be limited to fact finding and to advisory assistance. Its identity might vary from state to state, but it should always be an agency which has responsibility for some segment of public education in the state. Included among such organizations might be a state board of education, a state department of education, a state university, or a state public college. It should be made clear that such a study would be conducted without disruption of the schools. A report should be made to both the board of education and the staff. Alternatives to such an appeal procedure which have been tried include:

strikes, demagogic appeals, threats, withheld services, and sanctions or threatened sanctions by teachers;

withholding of contracts, blacklisting, failure of promotion, and other punitive action by school boards; and

yielding to undue influence of vested interests on the part of both school boards and teachers.

We believe that such arbitrary action by either staff or school board is not likely to lead to lasting and satisfying resolution of disagreements.[18]

The Role of the Personnel Administrator in the Power Structure

The personnel administrator works with all components in the power structure that has been discussed. Technically he is part of the administrative staff and yet, if he is to be effective, his role must be to try to keep each component in the power structure in a frame of reference so it can work with the others.

This might appear to suggest that he would be riding off in all directions, but actually it suggests that as the best-informed person on personnel relationships, he is in the best position to see and evaluate all sides of the question. His role in communication, interpretation, and evaluation of the issues is at a premium when working in the power structure made up of board, administration, and teaching personnel. He must be on one hand the advocate, representing the teaching personnel, and on the other hand the bargainer and staff administrator, representing the superintendent of schools.

In the final relationship his responsibility to the superintendent,

---

[18] American Association of School Administrators, *Roles, Responsibilities, Relationships of the School Board, Superintendent, and Staff* (Washington, D.C.: The Association, 1963), p. 14.

who in turn is responsible to the board, should permit him to maintain a reasonably flexible position while the going is rough.

The problem is to exercise the suggested mediation role and at the same time retain his effectiveness in the other aspects of personnel administration. Whether this is possible can only be determined by experience, which at this time is too limited to draw a firm conclusion.

CHAPTER VIII

Trends in School Personnel Administration

The trends in school personnel administration are inextricably associated with those in general school administration, which in turn is linked to the role of the school in society. Society is changing so rapidly that caution is suggested in noting trends and making predictions. Taking the year 1965 as a base point and looking at the changes since 1930 and considering the acceleration in social change now being experienced, the potential for change as one looks ahead to the year 2000 is overwhelming. Something of a shock is experienced when it is realized that the person employed as a new teacher in 1965, in all probability may still be teaching in the year 2000. How personnel policies can be geared to the expected changes to serve the school and such an employee is the challenge in trying to note trends. What seems important today may be only a passing event, or a mere part of a much larger context not now thoroughly understood. Therefore, in noting trends, only those things which represent fairly fundamental values will be noted. Out of such trends many changes in practices in school personnel administration will result; but it would be impractical, and probably subject to grave error, to try to predict these changes. The larger context of values will be used in venturing trends in school personnel administration.

Recognition of Democratic Procedures and Importance of Human Relations

It seems probable that this area may be cited as one of the directions for school personnel administration. It is not a new consideration and some may question its classification as a trend. However, like many educational practices, while it has received much attention in recent years, it is still only partially achieved in personnel administration. The practice of democratic procedures and good human relations in school personnel administration differ greatly in the school systems of the nation. There is great enlightenment in some school districts and extreme backwardness in others.

It seems plausible to consider this trend under the following headings, although admittedly they merge into each other in actual practice: (1) democratic aspects of school administration, (2) staff participation in policy making and planning, (3) human factors in personnel administration, and (4) increased employee organizational activity.

Democratic school administration. While used extensively in writings and discussions, no common meaning has been developed for this term. "Democratic" has usually been considered as an opposite to "authoritarian." Consequently, it is subject to all degrees of interpretation by administrators. What is democratic to some may be regarded as wholly unacceptable to others who operate within a different frame of reference. Some who accept the principle of democratic administration in theory reject it in practice.

The predicted trend is that a better understanding of the meaning of democratic school administration will emerge, with the perimeters of authority and participation better defined. As a result the areas in which boards, superintendents, principals, and teachers will work on policy matters will be better defined and delineated. This can come about only through maturation in the role concepts of those involved. A new generation of teachers and administrators, now being prepared, will give deeper and wider dimensions to this concept.

Staff participation in policy making and planning. Although well underway, this trend will see wholly new dimensions in the next few years, in the opinion of the writer. Unfortunately, the existing research in this area does not spell out the advantages, disadvantages, and limits of such participation, nor does it suggest effective organizational patterns for the involvement of staff in policy making and planning.

As viewed in practice in most school systems this activity has been related primarily to a means of communication, usually one way, from the board and administration to the staff.

There is a new direction to this activity in many enlightened school systems. It is the development of the activity in such a manner as to derive and bring to bear the knowledge, resourcefulness, and creativity of the entire staff upon the problems to be solved. Usually such programs are related to goal setting. If goals can be agreed upon, the matter of staff involvement in policy making and planning can be organized, implemented, and evaluated. The author has tentatively evolved the principles governing some of the methods, and inherent advantages, as well as the tentative limits of such participation in *Personnel Administration in Education*.[1] Further research is badly needed in this area. The author with others has defined the gaps between existing research and practice, as well as the additional research needs, in the course of a research project sponsored by the Cooperative Research Branch of the U.S. Office of Education. The scope of the problem is fully explored in this study.[2]

The extension of the concept of staff participation in policy making and planning is so involved with public policy that it seems likely to continue and be accelerated. It is viewed in this relationship in a recent study involving the social sciences and their contributions to the problems and practices in educational administration.[3]

Human factors in personnel administration. Personnel administration, as the name implies, involves people and their relationships. Increasingly school personnel administration, as well as other types of personnel administration, has been influenced by the growing acceptance that improvement in human relations in an organization is basic to accomplishing its purposes.

This change has been not altogether altruistic. It has come about partly as a result of a social revolution that has placed high value on the individual. It also results from the increasing complications in a mass society that have forced the use of human relations techniques. Cooperative, rather than manipulative, processes have proved to be superior in attaining organizational goals.

There have been extensive studies in this area, especially in business and industry, and more recently efforts have been made in school administration to study the problem. Griffiths states:

> Good human relations in a school system are built on a feeling of good will and mutual respect and faith in the dignity and worth of human beings as individual personalities. The administrator needs to develop skills in relating himself and others to the social setting

---

[1] Moore and Walters, *Personnel Administration in Education,* Chapters 2 and 3.

[2] Harold E. Moore, R. Merwin Deever, and Harold B. Hunnicutt, *High Priority Areas in School Personnel Administration* (Tempe, Arizona: Bureau of Educational Research and Services, Arizona State University, 1965).

[3] Donald E. Tope, *et al., The Social Sciences View School Administration* (Englewood Cliffs, N.J.: Prentice-Hall, Inc., 1965), Chapter 7.

in which he is placed. These skills are integral parts of the behavior of the administrator and may be developed and improved by an understanding of the content of human relations and by constant practice.

The content of human relations is concerned with the motives of man, communication, perception, power structure, authority, morale, group dynamics, decision-making, and leadership. Through the use of this substantive knowledge and practice in human relation situations, an administrator can develop skills which will make him more competent.[4]

Essentially the maintenance of desirable human relations involves the elimination of undesirable situations, the improvement of mutually desired situations, and the development of supporting situations. If these levels of consideration can be arrived at democratically through staff participation, the potential for improvement in human relations in an organization is greatly enhanced. The role of the personnel administrator as an expert in such processes is evident.

The area of human relations falls into the value concept frame of reference in the context in which trends in personnel administration are noted. The evidence is clear with respect to both the need for and the effort to improve human relations in school personnel practices.

Growing employee activity. The fourth facet of the recognition of democratic procedure and the importance of human relations is growing employee activity. At first thought this topic may seem not harmonious with the three that have been discussed. Some might consider it a cause and therefore not a parallel trend. However, growing employee activity has come about largely through the increased use of democratic procedures in school administration and the practice of better human relations. Some of the aspects of employee activity have been discussed in Chapter VII. The trend of increasing militancy on the part of the organized staff was noted. As a relatively new dimension of school personnel administration, collective action by teacher groups is forcing a re-assessment of policies and in some cases laws themselves, governing the relations of teacher organizations, administrators, and boards of education.

It is difficult to assess a trend while in the midst of it. However, if the example of what has happened in business and industry can be

---

[4] Daniel E. Griffiths, *Human Relations in School Administration* (New York: Appleton-Century-Crofts, 1956), pp. 19–20.

used, the increase in employee activity will accelerate and not dimin-
ish. The trend should be characterized by better definition of roles,
clearer understanding of responsibility on the part of those concerned, and a willingness to accept the consequences of the "partner-
ship" role in policy making and planning in the school organization.

The conflict between teacher organizations growing out of the difference of opinion in the philosophical outlook of the role of the
teacher is an area which must soon be resolved. It is clearly a part
of the trend in the sense that it is a current issue.

Another current issue, only beginning to be assessed, is the relationship of growing employee activity upon the teaching-learning
situation. One of the other trends in personnel administration is to
try to find ways and means of evaluating the effect of the growing
militancy of the staff upon the basic purposes of the public school.
As previously noted, the contemporary nature of the problem with
respect to growing employee activity makes it difficult to know just
where to place the problem in the spectrum of trends.

Effective Use of Personnel Resources

The more effective use of the personnel force is clearly a trend in
school personnel administration. Faced by a continuing shortage of
highly qualified personnel, especially in certain specialized fields, the
increasing costs of education and the greater demands by the public
upon the schools and consequently upon the staff, how to deploy the
staff effectively becomes a major problem.

Increasingly it appears necessary to classify and describe the jobs
to be done in order to relate the personnel services to them. In
Chapter II of this text the author referred to the importance of job
classifications and descriptions for all school employees. It appears
that this is a primary consideration in deploying staff effectively.

Assignments should take into consideration the necessary qualifications for the job to be done. If persons are assigned who do not
have the necessary qualifications, the job will suffer. If persons of
higher than necessary qualifications are assigned, the persons involved, the economics of the situation, and the morale of the staff
suffer. The trend is to fit the person and the qualifications to the job
requirements. Often this means assigning certain activities normally
associated with a job to others. For example, the teacher's activities

that are strictly clerical should be performed by persons with clerical qualifications. On the other hand there may be activities that the teacher will need the help of specialists in performing.

The need for continued research and experimentation in this area is clear in order to resolve the limits of the teacher's activities.

Functioning in an Atmosphere of Conflict and Unrest

One of the unhappy trends in school personnel administration is its necessity to function in an atmosphere of conflict and unrest. However, this situation can be used constructively to provide for progress if the problem is viewed and worked upon in a positive context.

At the outset of the chapter it was noted that it was impossible to separate personnel administration from general school administration and the latter from society itself.

Nearly twenty years ago the author heard the late Edward R. Murrow in an address to the American Council on Education say that one of the problems of our day was to learn to live with conflict. He said, pointing to the ideological conflict between communism and democracy, that for the next twenty, thirty, forty, or fifty years this would be a characteristic of the society. The atmosphere of general conflict has permeated many aspects of society, including staff relations. Learning to live with these conditions and at the same time function effectively is one of the current challenges. If handled constructively it involves developing goals based on values, evolving principles to give them structure, and practices harmonious with the goals and principles.

This trend calls for a highly professional approach that will permit an impersonal yet very human approach to a solution of the issues.

It also involves a constant effort on the part of the personnel administrator, working with others, to retain the image of the teacher and other personnel as professionals, in order to retain the support of the public for education. This involves a program of interpretation that will place the schools in proper perspective in a changing society, thus portraying them as institutions that would lose their effectiveness if seen apart from the social scene. There is no other current issue with a greater challenge.

The Trend to Use Research Findings

Fortunately one of the current trends in personnel administration is to put increasing dependence upon research. In a field where research has been limited and where there has been a wide gap between existing research and practice, the increasing use of this important tool holds promise. The development of research in the personnel area has paralleled the development of research in the behavioral sciences. In fact, many of the research methods and techniques are borrowed from this field and adapted to personnel administration. Illustrations may be found in studies of morale, values and value perception, leadership practices, role perception, and others.

The need in the research area can be classified under two general areas: (1) bridging the gap between research and practice, and (2) identifying the need for, and conducting, new research. While not a movement in the sense that a great deal has been accomplished, there is sufficient interest to justify indicating these as promising trends.

Bridging the gap between research and practice. Some of the useful means and procedures in bridging the gap between research and practice include:

—A system for classifying research in school personnel administration.

—Wider dissemination and interpretation of research findings.

—Greater use of research findings in training programs and actual practice.

—Published annotated bibliographies and a regular publication devoted to school personnel.

—Identification of an agency to foster, classify, and disseminate personnel research.

—Identification and support of a center to specialize in personnel research.

—Close cooperation between such a center and a group of co-operating school districts which could serve as laboratories.

—Local organizations of school districts, such as study councils, to encourage and cooperate in personnel research and to improve practice.

—Greater use of the research resources in universities by school districts.

—Better support of research in local school districts, enabling local personnel administrators to avail themselves of research services.

—Exchange programs between the university staff which teaches and conducts personnel research and practicing personnel staff from cooperating school districts.

—Improved local recording of problems where research help is needed.

Identifying and conducting research. There would be unlimited opportunities in the personnel area if funds and qualified staff were available. A few personnel areas have been selected and some of the research needs identified. Most of the areas are related to the current trends in personnel activities that have been identified in this chapter.

Research needs in policy making and planning. Some of the needs in this area are:

—Comparison of the advantages and disadvantages of staff participation in policy making and planning.

—Determination of the roles of staff members, administrators, and school board members as related to such participation.

—Studies in communication as it operates upward and downward in the hierarchy of the educational staff.

—Determination of the most effective methods of selecting staff to serve in representative relationships in policy making and planning procedures.

Research needs in leadership development and selection. Representative needs in this area for research are:

—Determination of the effectiveness of typical school administrative training programs.

—Development of instruments and procedures to aid administrators in the selection of leaders and in leadership development.

—Determination of which areas of graduate and undergraduate studies are most useful in preparing personnel administrators.

—Investigations into the place of interdisciplinary content in such training programs.

—Determination of the appropriate administrative duties and activities in the various administrative positions.

—Studies in the internal (within the individual) and the external (within the organization) strains in the several administrative job relationships.

Research in the role and relationship of teacher organizations. Some of the studies needed in this area are:

—Determination of what matters are subject to negotiations in teacher organization-school board relationships.

—Determination of how these negotiable matters vary depending upon the type of teacher organization.

—Determination of the effective role of teacher organizations in planning and decision making in curriculum development and methodology.

—Determination of the effect of the use of power tactics by teacher organizations on the public image of the teacher.

—Studies in the unity or cohesiveness of the staff before and after engaging in a collective action.

—Determination of the extent to which teachers and their organizations are ready, willing, and able to assume the responsibility for the results of their collective action in such fields as curriculum, teaching methodology, and child welfare.

Research needs in teacher morale. A few of the many needed research areas in this field are:

—The development of new methodology, techniques, and instruments for effectively measuring and appraising teacher morale.

—Studies in determining the relationship of teacher morale to pupil achievement.

—Additional studies on the effect of the various types of pay scales, including "merit" pay upon teacher morale.

—Studies in the effect on teacher morale when most of the non-teaching duties are re-assigned to supporting staff.

—Studies in the relationship between teacher morale and load.

—Studies in relationship between teacher morale and community status of teachers.

—Studies in the relationship between teacher morale and the levels of community financial support of education.

Research needs in conceptual framework for school personnel administration. There are many fundamental areas needing research in this field as it pertains to personnel administration. A few of them are:

—Identification and definition of goals and values affecting school personnel administration.

—The identification and definition of existing educational values.

—Determination of the effects of different personnel policies upon the achievement of value goals.

—Determination of the levels at which decisions affecting personnel administration are actually made.

—Determination of the modifications that are necessary in decision making procedures because of the growing militancy of teachers.

—Determination of the source of evidence used by administrators in decision making in personnel administration.

Conclusions. Considerable emphasis has been given to research at the end of this book because of its importance and the promising trend to use it more extensively in improving personnel administration.

This trend will have permanent effect only as personnel administrators assume a research role in their jobs, utilize existing research, and insist that their colleagues also operate from a base of sound research information, if it is available.

The basic function of research in personnel administration should be the improvement of the teaching-learning situation. Thus we return to the basic purpose of personnel administration, which is accomplishing the educational objectives of the school system as set forth in the introduction to Chapter I.

Bibliography

American Association of School Administrators, *The American School Superintendency*, 30th Yearbook. Washington, D.C.: The Association, 1952.

————, *Roles, Responsibilities, Relationships of the School Board, Superintendent, and Staff*. Washington, D.C.: The Association, 1963.

————, *Staff Relations in School Administration*. Washington, D.C.: The Association, 1951.

American Educational Research Association, "Teacher Personnel," *Review of Educational Research*, XXXIII, No. 4, October 1963, Washington, D.C.: The Association, 1963.

Campbell, Roald F., and Russell T. Gregg, eds., *Administrative Behavior in Education*. New York: Harper & Row, Publishers, Inc., 1957.

Elsbree, Willard S., E. Edmund Reutter, Jr., and Associates, *Principles of Staff Personnel Administration*. New York: Bureau of Publications, Teachers College, Columbia University, 1959.

Gauerke, Warren E., *School Law*. New York: The Center for Applied Research in Education, Inc., 1965.

Gibson, R. Oliver, and Herold C. Hunt, *The School Personnel Administrator*. Boston: Houghton Mifflin Company, 1965.

Griffiths, Daniel E., *Administrative Theory*. New York: Appleton-Century-Crofts, 1959.

————, *Human Relations in School Administration*. New York: Appleton-Century-Crofts, 1956.

Jenson, Theodore J., and David L. Clark, *Educational Administration*. New York: The Center for Applied Research in Education, Inc., 1964.

Kindred, Leslie W., and Prince B. Woodard, *Staff Welfare Practices in the Public Schools*. New York: The Center for Applied Research in Education, Inc., 1963.

Megel, Carl J., *Collective Bargaining Contracts*. Chicago: The American Federation of Teachers, 1963.

Mitzel, Harold E., "Teacher Effectiveness," *Encyclopedia of Educational Research*. New York: The Macmillan Company, 1960.

Moffitt, John Clifton, *In-Service Education for Teachers*. New York: The Center for Applied Research in Education, Inc., 1963.

Moore, Harold E., and John E. Burke, "Staff-Economic Status," *Encyclopedia of Educational Research*. New York: The Macmillan Company, 1960.

Moore, Harold E., R. Merwin Deever, and Harold B. Nunnicutt, *High Priority Areas in School Personnel Administration*. Tempe, Arizona: Bureau of Educational Research and Services, Arizona State University, 1965.

Moore, Harold E., and Newell B. Walters, *Personnel Administration in Education.* New York: Harper & Rowe, Publishers, 1955.

National Education Association, *Implementing the Code of Ethics of the Education Profession and Strengthening Professional Rights.* Washington, D.C.: The Association, 1964.

————, National Commission on Professional Rights and Responsibilities, *Guidelines for Professional Sanctions.* Washington, D.C.: The Association, 1963.

————, Office of Professional Development and Welfare, *Guidelines for Professional Negotiations,* rev. ed., Washington, D.C.: The Association, 1965.

————, Research Division, *Evaluation of Classroom Teachers.* Washington, D.C.: The Association, 1964.

————, ————, *Index Salary Schedules for Classroom Teachers, 1964–65, Research Memo 1965–6.* Washington, D.C.: The Association, March 1965.

————, ————, *The Morale of Teachers* (prepared by Dr. Frederick C. Redefer), Research Memo, 1963–18 (Washington, D.C.: The Association, 1963).

————, ————, *The Public School Personnel Administrator,* Research Monograph 1962–M1 (Washington, D.C.: The Association, 1962).

————, ————, *Professional Negotiations with School Boards: A Legal Analysis and Review* (Washington, D.C.: The Association, January 1962).

————, ————, *Salary Schedules for Classroom Teachers, 1964–65,* Research Report 1964–E13 (Washington, D.C.: The Association, March 1965).

————, Educational Policies Commission, *The Unique Role of the Superintendent of Schools.* Washington, D.C.: The Association, 1955.

National Society for the Study of Education, *Behavioral Science and Educational Administration,* 63rd Yearbook. Chicago: The University of Chicago Press, 1964.

Staehle, John F., *Characteristics of Administrative Handbooks for School Staff Personnel.* Bulletin 1960, No. 13, Office of Education, Washington, D.C.: Superintendent of Documents, U.S. Government Printing Office, 1960.

Steffensen, James P., *Merit Salary Programs,* Office of Education Bulletin 1963, No. 5. Washington, D.C.: Superintendent of Documents, U.S. Government Printing Office, 1963.

Tope, Donald E. *et al., The Social Sciences View School Administration.* Englewood Cliffs, N.J.: Prentice-Hall, Inc., 1965.

Van Zwoll, James A., *School Personnel Administration.* New York: Appleton-Century-Crofts, 1964.

Wildman, Wesley A., "Collective Action by Public School Teachers," *Industrial and Labor Relations Review,* XVIII, No. 1, October 1964.

————, "Implications of Teacher Bargaining for Administrators," *Phi Delta Kappan,* XLVI, No. 4, December 1964.

Index

Index